MARGARET THATCHER

Books LLC®, Reference Series, Memphis, USA, 2011. ISBN: 9781156096918. www.booksllc.net. Copyright: http://creativecommons.org/licenses/by-sa/3.0/deed.en

Table of Contents

1990 Prime Minister's Resignation Honours	2
Aftermath of the Falklands War	3
Blatcherism	7
Bruges Group	7
Carol Thatcher	8
Centre for Policy Studies	9
Conservative Party (UK) leadership election, 1975	10
Conservative Party (UK) leadership election, 1989	11
Conservative Party (UK) leadership election, 1990	11
Denis Thatcher	13
Electoral history of Margaret Thatcher	15
Falklands War	16
Finchley (UK Parliament constituency)	27
Iron Lady	27
Maggie Out	28
Margaret Thatcher	29
Mark Thatcher	38
Premiership of Margaret Thatcher	39
Public Bodies (Admission to Meetings) Act 1960	48
Sanctuary (Iron Maiden song)	49
Shops Bill 1986	49
Statecraft: Strategies for a Changing World	50
Thatcher's England	50
Thatcher ministry	51
Thatcherism	53
There Is No Alternative: Why Margaret Thatcher Matters	57
There is no alternative	58
United Kingdom general election, 1979	58
United Kingdom general election, 1983	59
United Kingdom general election, 1987	61
University of Buckingham	62
Westland affair	66

Introduction

Purchase of this book entitles you to a free trial membership in the publisher's book club at www.booksllc.net. (Time limited offer.) Simply enter the barcode number from the back cover onto the membership form. The book club entitles you to select from hundreds of thousands of books at no additional charge. You can also download a digital copy of this and related books to read on the go. Simply enter the title or subject onto the search form to find them.

Each chapter in this book ends with a URL to a hyperlinked online version. Type the URL exactly as it appears. If you change the URL's capitalization it won't work. Use the online version to access related pages, websites, footnotes, tables, color photos, updates. Click the version history tab to see the chapter's contributors. Click the edit link to suggest changes.

A large and diverse editor base collaboratively wrote the book, not a single author. After a long process of discussion and debate, the chapters gradually took on a neutral point of view reached through consensus. Additional editors expanded and contributed to chapters striving to achieve balance and comprehensive coverage. This reduced the regional or cultural bias found in many other books and provided access and breadth on subject matter otherwise little documented.

1990 Prime Minister's Resignation Honours

Margaret Thatcher

The **1990 Prime Minister's Resignation Honours** were officially announced in the *London Gazette* of 21 December 1990 and marked the November 1990 resignation of Prime Minister Margaret Thatcher.

Life Peers

- Dame Joan Seccombe, DBE, Vice Chairman, Conservative Party.
- Professor Brian Griffiths, formerly Special Advisor to Margaret Thatcher, and Head of Policy Unit.
- Sir Hector Laing, Life President, United Biscuits (Holdings) plc.
- Peter Garth Palumbo, Chairman, Arts Council of Great Britain.
- Sir Jeffrey Maurice Sterling, CBE, Chairman, the Peninsular and Oriental Steam Navigation Company, Vice Chairman and Chairman of the Executive, Motability.
- Sir (Vincent) Gordon Lindsay White, KBE, Chairman, Hanson Industries.
- Sir David Wolfson, Chairman, Haigside Ltd.

Knights Bachelor

- Timothy John Leigh Bell, Deputy Chairman, Lowe Bell Communications.
- George Arthur Gardiner, MP, Member of Parliament for Reigate.
- Bernard Ingham, formerly Chief Press Secretary, 10 Downing Street.
- Geoffrey Norman Leigh, Chairman, Allied London Properties plc.
- Nicholas Markley Lloyd, Editor, *Daily Express*.
- The Rt. Hon. Peter Hugh Morrison, MP, Member of Parliament for the City of Chester. Deputy Chairman, Conservative Party 1986–1989. Lately Parliamentary Private Secretary, 10 Downing Street.
- Gerrard Anthony Neale, MP, Member of Parliament for North Cornwall.
- Michael Jon Neubert, MP, Member of Parliament for Romford. Formerly Parliamentary Under Secretary of State for the Armed Forces.

Order of the Bath

Companions (CB)

- Andrew Turnbull, Principal Private Secretary, Prime Minister's Office, 10 Downing Street.

Order of St Michael and St George

Knights Commander (KCMG)

- Charles David Powell, Private Secretary, Prime Minister's Office, 10 Downing Street.

Order of the British Empire

Dames Commander (DBE)

- Jane Elizabeth Gow, for political and public service.
- Sue Tinson, Associate Editor, Independent Television News.

Commanders (CBE)

- John Robin Catforo, Secretary for Appointments, Prime Minister's Office, 10 Downing Street.
- Joan Valerie Hall, Member Council, University College of Buckingham. Formerly Member of Parliament for Keighley 1970–1974.
- Dr. John Henderson, Personal Physician to Margaret Thatcher
- Brian Hitchen, Editor, *Daily Star*.
- Olga Polizzi, Member, Westminster City Council.
- (John) Harvey Noake Thomas, International Public Relations Consultant: Consultant Director of Presentation and Promotion, Conservative Party.

Officers (OBE)

- Marjorie Sherman. For charitable services.
- Christine Margaret Wall, Head of News Department, Conservative Central Office.
- John Flasby Lawrance Whittingdale, formerly Political Secretary; Prime Minister's Office, 10 Downing Street.

Members (MBE)

- Jean Dibblin, Senior Personal Secretary, Prime Minister's Office, 10 Downing Street.
- Susan Irene Goodchild, Invitations Secretary, Prime Minister's Office, 10 Downing Street.
- Dorothy Haynes, Curator/Housekeeper at Chequers.
- Margaret King, Fashion Director, Aquascutum Ltd.
- Robert "Bob" Kingston, Personal Detective to Margaret Thatcher
- Amanda Ponsonby, formerly Personal Assistant to Margaret Thatcher
- Janice Kay Richards, Head of Garden Rooms, Prime Minister's Office, 10 Downing Street.
- Sherry Dorelia Warner, Senior Cook, Prime Minister's Office, 10 Downing Street.

British Empire Medal (BEM)

- Edwina Mary Booker, Cleaner, Prime Minister's Office, 10 Downing Street.
- Alma Dew, Telephonist, Prime Minister's Office, 10 Downing Street.
- Sergeant Theresa Maria Duda, Women's Royal Air Force. Assistant

House Manager at Chequers.
- Peter Paul D'Emanuele, Messenger, Prime Minister's Office, 10 Downing Street.
- Alfred George Frederick Heath, Custody Guard Supervisor, Prime Minister's Office, 10 Downing Street.
- Doris Agnes "Dot" King, Messenger. Prime Minister's Office, 10 Downing Street.
- Anthony James Robert Yandle, Deputy House Manager, Prime Minister's Office, 10 Downing Street.

Source (edited): "http://en.wikipedia.org/wiki/1990_Prime_Minister%27s_Resignation_Honours"

Aftermath of the Falklands War

Political aftermath

Diplomatic relations between the UK and Argentina were not restored until 1989 under a formula which put the issue of sovereignty to one side (*the sovereignty umbrella*) and established a framework within which further talks on matters of mutual interest could be held

Argentina

The Argentine loss of the war led to ever-larger protests against the military regime and is credited with giving the final push to drive out the military government that had overthrown Isabel Perón in 1976 and participated in the crimes of the Dirty War. Galtieri was forced to resign and elections were held on 30 October 1983 and a new president, Raúl Alfonsín, the Radical Civic Union (UCR) party candidate, took office on 10 December 1983, defeating Italo Luder, the candidate for the Justicialist Party (Peronist movement). In the long term the debacle concluded the periodical intervention of the Argentine military in the politics since the 1930s.

Mobilisation of national identity in Argentina, called the "Malvinas Spirit," has now developed in a constant recovery of the relevant aspects of the war that boost national self-image.

In 2009, Argentine authorities in Comodoro Rivadavia ratified a decision made by authorities in Río Grande, Tierra del Fuego (which, according to Argentina, have authority over the islands) charging 70 officers and corporals with inhumane treatment of conscript soldiers during the war."We have testimony from 23 people about a soldier who was shot to death by a corporal, four other former combatants who starved to death, and at least 15 cases of conscripts who were staked out on the ground," Pablo Vassel, under-secretary of human rights in the province of Corrientes, told Inter Press Service News Agency. There are claims that false testimonies were used as evidence in accusing the Argentine officers and NCOs and Vassel had to step down from his post as under-secretary of human rights of Corrientes in 2010.

The Falkland Islands

The Falkland Islands remained a self governing British overseas territory, but shortly after the war the Islanders gained British Citizenship (replacing British Dependent Territories citizenship), strengthening the link between the Islanders and the UK.

The economy also benefited indirectly from UK military investment and directly from development of fisheries. The future of the Falkland Islanders' link to the UK has been more certain as a result of the war, and the Islands' government remains committed to self-determination and British sovereignty.

United Kingdom

For the UK, the war cost 255 men, six ships (ten others suffered varying degrees of battle damage), 34 aircraft and £2.778 billion, but the campaign was considered a great victory for the United Kingdom. The war provided a substantial boost to the popularity of Margaret Thatcher and undoubtedly played a role in ensuring her re-election in 1983. Several members of her government resigned however, including the Foreign Secretary Lord Carrington, the most recent time that a UK government minister resigned openly in response to a failure of his department (in not anticipating the war).

Criticism was levelled at Ted Rowlands, a former junior foreign minister in the preceding government, who disclosed in Parliament in April 1982 that the British had broken the Argentine diplomatic codes. As the same code machines were used by the Argentine military, this disclosure immediately served to deny British access to valuable intelligence. This, and other responses to parliamentary questions, and leaks of information to the BBC has been alleged by historian Hugh Bicheno to be a deliberate attempt to undermine the Thatcher government on the part of a variety of individuals who had a vested interest in its fall. There is some debate as to the accuracy of the claims regarding Ted Rowland. Mark Urban in his book *UK Eyes Alpha* makes reference to a "figure intimate with the workings of GCHQ" who suggested that Rowlands's comment had no noticeable effect.

Ultimately, the successful conclusion of the war gave a noticeable fillip to British patriotic feeling, with the mobilisation of national identity encapsulated in the so-called "Falklands Factor". Since the failure of the 1956 Suez campaign, the end of Empire and the economic decline of the 1970s which culminated in the Winter of Discontent, Britain had been beset by uncertainty and anxiety about its international role, status and capability. With the war successfully concluded, Thatcher was returned to power with an increased Parliamentary majority and felt empowered to press ahead with the economic readjustments of Thatcherism. A second major effect was a reaffirmation of the special relationship between the US and UK. Both Reagan and Weinberger (his Secretary of Defense) were appointed honorary Knights Commander of the Order of the British Empire (KBE) for their help in the campaign, but the more obvious result was the common alignment of Britain and the USA in a more confrontational foreign policy against the Soviet bloc, sometimes known as the Second Cold War.

In 2007 the British government expressed regrets over the deaths on both sides in the war. Margaret Thatcher was quoted as saying "in the struggle against evil... we can all today draw hope and strength" from the Falklands victory, while former Argentinian President Néstor Kirchner claimed while in office that the UK won a colonial victory and vowed that the islands would one day return to Argentine sovereignty. He augmented this however, with an affirmation that the use of force could never again be used in an attempt to bring this about.

USA and Latin America
The United States' reputation in parts of Latin America was damaged because of the perception that it had broken the Rio Treaty (Inter-American Treaty of Reciprocal Assistance or TIAR) by providing the UK with military supplies.

In September 2001 the President of Mexico Vicente Fox cited the Falklands War as proof of the failure of the TIAR.

Regarding the attitude of the Latin American governments, K.J. Holsti presents another sight of the South American dilemma: *"While South American governments (except Chile) publicly supported Argentina in its conflict with Great Britain, in private many governments were pleased with the outcome of the war. Argentina's bellicosity against Chile over the Beagle Channel problem ... [its] foreign intervention ([in] Bolivia and Nicaragua) ... and [its] propounded geopolitical doctrines that were seen in other countries as threatening to them".* So, according to David R. Mares, *"Brazilian military analysts worried about the problems of having a successful and belligerent Argentina as neighbour"*.

For Chile, engaged with Argentina in a long standing territorial dispute over the Cape Horn islands, the outcome of the war averted a planned Argentine military invasion of Chile and made possible the Treaty of Peace and Friendship of 1984 between Chile and Argentina.

The visit of Pope John Paul II
In May 1982, Pope John Paul II carried out a long-scheduled visit to the United Kingdom. In view of the crisis it was decided that this should be balanced with an unscheduled trip to Argentina in June. It is contended that his presence and words spiritually prepared Argentines for a possible defeat, contrary to the propaganda issued by the Junta. He returned to Argentina in 1987 after the return of democratic government.

Military analysis
Militarily, the Falklands conflict remains the largest air-naval combat operation between modern forces since the end of the Second World War. As such, it has been the subject of intense study by military analysts and historians. The most significant "lessons learned" include: the vulnerability of surface ships to anti-ship missiles and submarines, the challenges of coordinating logistical support for a long-distance projection of power, and reconfirmation of the role of tactical air power, including the use of helicopters.

Vulnerability of surface ships
In his book *The Price of Admiralty,* military historian Sir John Keegan noted that the brief conflict showed the irremediable vulnerability of surface ships to anti-ship missiles, and, most importantly, to submarines: despite the seemingly limited consequences of the war, it confirmed the dominance of the submarine in naval warfare. This is especially so, Keegan argues, because submarines are far less vulnerable than aircraft to counterattack, being able to approach and destroy their targets with almost complete impunity. However, many prominent naval tacticians have recently argued this point; the sinking of the ARA *General Belgrano* was a result of a pre-WWII ship with no anti-submarine capabilities against a modern nuclear-powered submarine and the various British ships sunk by the Argentinian Air Force were acceptable in the fact that they were screen forces for the British aircraft carriers.

Role of air power
Neither side achieved total air supremacy; nonetheless, air power proved to be of critical importance during the conflict, due to the isolated, rough landscape of the Falklands in which the mobility of land forces was restricted. Air strikes were staged against ground, sea and air targets on both sides, and often with clear results. All of the UK losses at sea were caused by aircraft or missile strikes (by both the Argentine Air Force and Naval Aviation). The French Exocet missile proved its lethality in air-to-surface operations, leading to retrofitting of most major ships with Close-in weapon systems (CIWS).

The air war in the Falklands vindicated the UK decision to maintain at least the STOVL aircraft carriers after the retirement of HMS *Ark Royal*. The domination of air power in major naval engagements was demonstrated, along with the usefulness of carriers and it proved the small but manoeuvrable Sea Harrier as a true fighter. Sea Harriers shot down 21 aircraft with no air-to-air losses themselves, although six were lost to ground fire and accidents.

It should be noted that the disparity in figures, with the Argentine fighters failing to shoot down a single Sea Harrier, can be explained by several factors. The air combat training of the British pilots was indisputably superior; limited fighter control was provided by British warships in San Carlos Water, the then almost unparalleled Blue Fox radar, and the extreme manoeuvrability of the Sea Harrier. Additionally the British had the latest AIM-9L Sidewinder missiles, while the only Argentine planes with air-to-air missiles for self defence were the Mirages. The AIM-9Ls had a much wider angle of engagement than the earlier versions employed by the Argentines, which could only effectively engage the rear quarter of an enemy aircraft. The only advantage of the Argentine jets was their higher maximum speed, but Argentine pilots could not benefit from this unless they risked running out of fuel, as was seen in the first air combat of the war when a Mirage IIIEA was forced to attempt a landing at

Stanley.

The importance of Airborne Early Warning (AEW) was shown. The Royal Navy had effectively no over-the-horizon radar capability. This was hastily rectified after the war, with Sea King helicopters fitted with radomes containing a variant of the Nimrod ASW aircraft's Searchwater radar. These first travelled south after the war on the brand new HMS *Illustrious*, sister ship to *Invincible*.

The usefulness of helicopters in combat, logistic, and casevac operations was confirmed.

Logistics

The logistical capability of the UK armed forces was stretched to the absolute limit in order to mount an amphibious operation so far from a land base, in mountainous islands with few roads. After the war much work was done to improve both the logistical and amphibious capability of the Royal Navy. Task force commander Rear Admiral Sir Sandy Woodward refers to the conflict as "a lot closer run than many would care to believe", reflecting the naval and military belief that few people understood—or understand—the extent to which the logistical dimension made the war a difficult operation for the UK. The ships of the task force could only remain on station for a limited time in the worsening southern hemisphere winter. With such a high proportion of the Royal Navy's surface fleet actively engaged, or lost in combat, there were few units available for northbound traffic. At the core of the fleet, *Invincible* could possibly have been replaced by the hastily-prepared *Illustrious*, but there was no replacement available for *Hermes*, the larger of the two British carriers. Woodward's strategy, therefore, required the land war to be won before *Hermes*, in particular, succumbed to the harsh environment. Woodward called the operation "a damned close-run thing", quoting the Duke of Wellington after the Battle of Waterloo.

Special forces

The usefulness of special forces units was reaffirmed. British special forces destroyed many Argentine aircraft (notably in the SAS raid on Pebble Island) and carried out highly informative intelligence-gathering operations. Contrary to popular understanding, the Argentine special forces also patrolled hard, in appalling climatic conditions, against a professional enemy and showed that they could sometimes get the upper hand.

Nylon was shown to be a poor choice for fabric in uniforms, as it is more flammable than cotton and also melts with heat. Burning nylon adheres to the skin, causing avoidable casualties.

Impact on the Royal Navy

Strained by two oil crises (1973 and 1979), the United Kingdom's government desired to cut defence spending in line with the rest of Europe. Many former British possessions in Africa and Asia had gained independence from the UK by the 1980s. Due to this decolonisation, successive British governments investigated closing British overseas bases and reducing the UK's armed forces in the belief that capabilities such as a blue water navy were no longer required. The Conservative government's Defence Secretary John Nott produced a white paper in 1981 proposing major cuts for the navy in the next ten years (the army and the RAF had already been tailored for NATO.)

Denis Healey, the Defence Secretary in 1966, once said that aircraft carriers were required only for operations regarding 'landing or withdrawal of troops against sophisticated opposition outside range of land-based air cover'. When the last conventional carrier in the Royal Navy, HMS *Ark Royal*, was decommissioned in 1978, the pro-carrier lobby succeeded in acquiring light carriers (euphemistically christened 'through deck cruisers') equipped with VTOL Sea Harriers as well as helicopters, justified by the fact that one of their primary roles was anti-submarine warfare. John Nott's defence review concluded that anti-submarine defence would be performed more cheaply by a smaller number of destroyers and frigates. The carrier HMS *Hermes* was therefore to be scrapped and HMS *Invincible* sold to Australia. Under the review, the Royal Navy was focussed primarily on anti-submarine warfare under the auspices of NATO. Any out-of-area amphibious operations were considered unlikely. The entire Royal Marines was in jeopardy of being disbanded and the sale of HMS *Intrepid* and HMS *Fearless* was mooted.

In 1980 low funding caused many ships to be in harbour for months due to lack of spare parts and fuel. The largest cut in the Royal Navy's conventional forces led to the resignation of the Navy Minister Keith Speed in 1981. Sea battles, mass convoys, amphibious landings and coastal bombardments were considered obsolete in the second half of the 20th century. The head of the admiralty, First Sea Lord Admiral Sir Henry Leach was still fighting the cuts in the Ministry of Defence together with the Chief of Defence Staff, who by chance, was also a naval officer — Admiral of the Fleet Sir Terence Lewin.

At the onset of the crisis, First Sea Lord Sir Henry Leach was summoned to brief the Prime Minister. He claimed that Britain was able to recapture the islands, and that it should be done. "Since here was a clear, imminent threat to British overseas territory that could only be reached by sea, what the hell was the point in having a Navy if it was not used for this sort of thing?". Aware of the necessity for speed, Leach had already given orders for the ships of a potential task force to be prepared for deployment. On 2 April, at a briefing at the House of Commons, Leach advised the Prime Minister that a task force was necessary and could sail within 48 hours. Lewin, who was forced to return from a scheduled visit to New Zealand also impressed on the War Cabinet that the primary objective for the United Kingdom should be: "to bring about the withdrawal of Argentine forces from the Falkland Islands, and the re-establishment of British administration there, as quickly as possible". Inspired, Thatcher ordered the despatch of the Task Force for the South Atlantic.

After the war, the sale of HMS *Invin-*

cible to Australia was cancelled, with *Hermes* offered instead (eventually being sold to India as INS *Viraat* in 1986), and the operational status of all three support carriers was maintained. The proposed cutback in the surface fleet was abandoned and replacements for many of the lost ships and helicopters plus more Sea Harriers were ordered. The amphibious assault ships HMS *Fearless* and HMS *Intrepid* were not decommissioned until 2002 and 1999 respectively, being replaced by HMS *Albion* and HMS *Bulwark*. The Royal Navy confirmed its commitment to a carrier force with the order of two Queen Elizabeth class carriers in 2007.

Soviet Union/Warsaw Pact

For the Soviet/Warsaw Pact militaries, the Falklands War forced a re-examination of their estimates of the quality of Western troops, and particularly how all-volunteer forces compared with conscripted forces. The Soviets were aware that the British relied heavily on the quality and training of its personnel to compensate for the extreme logistical difficulties the campaign presented, and also noted that both sides were using many of the same weapons systems.

Weapon export controls

The Coordinating Committee for Multilateral Export Controls (COCOM) failed to anticipate a conflict between Argentina and the UK when approving weapon exports to Argentina.

Allegations of nuclear deployment

It has been reported that two years after the war, Labour MPs demanded an inquiry into reports that a Resolution class submarine armed with the Polaris SLBMs had deployed to Ascension Island during the operation, ostensibly to prepare for a nuclear strike. The Ministry of Defence is reported to have denied the allegations, and Freedman's Official History does the same.

In 1982, British warships were routinely armed with the WE.177, a tactical nuclear weapon with a variable yield of either 10 kilotons or 0.5 kiloton, which was used as a Nuclear Depth Bomb in an antisubmarine role. The Official History describes the contorted logistical arrangements that led to the removal of the nuclear depth bombs from the frigates, following political alarm in Whitehall. Eventually at least some of the depth bombs were brought back to the UK by an RFA vessel. In December 2003, Argentine President Néstor Kirchner demanded an apology from the British Government for this "regrettable and monstrous" act.

Intelligence analysis

MI6 activity

In his 2002 memoirs Sir John Nott, Britain's Secretary of State for Defence during the conflict, made the following disclosure regarding the activities of the UK's Secret Intelligence Service (MI6): I authorised our agents to pose as bona fide purchasers of equipment on the international market, ensuring that we outbid the Argentines, and other agents identified Exocet missiles in markets and rendered them inoperable.

Norwegian intelligence

According to a documentary by the Norwegian Broadcasting Corporation (NRK), during the war a Norwegian Intelligence Service facility situated at Fauske in the northern county of Nordland regularly intercepted Soviet satellite intelligence data, which was forwarded to the Northwood Headquarters. Said "a high ranking British military source":
When the war broke out, we ourselves almost didn't have any intelligence information from this area. It was here we got help from the Norwegians, who gave us a stream of information about the Argentine warships' positions. The information came to us all the time and straight to our war headquarters at Northwood. The information was continuously updated and told us exactly where the Argentine ships were.

Soviet intervention

According to Russian journalist Sergei Brilev, whose claims were reported in *The Times* on 2 April 2010, Argentina may have received satellite imagery of British dispositions from the Soviet Union during the conflict.

Legal

70 Argentine military officers are currently accused of crimes against humanity for the alleged abuse, torture and, in one case, murder of their own troops.

Medical

Survival and recovery of wounded British soldiers

During the operations, several wounded British soldiers had to spend hours in the cold before receiving medical aid—yet no British soldier died who was evacuated to a medical aid station, a fact confirmed by Surgeon Commander Rick Jolly, the Medical Officer In Charge of the refrigeration plant at Ajax Bay (nicknamed "The Red and Green Life machine" by the medics). Many recovered better than medical opinion of the time considered possible, and subsequent theories have suggested that this was due to the extreme cold. Britain also had medical staff familiar with high velocity gunshot wounds, due to their experiences in the Northern Ireland conflict with the IRA.

Medical and psychological treatment of Falklands veterans

The British Ministry of Defence was accused several times of a systematic failure to prepare service personnel for the horrors of war and to provide adequate care for them afterwards.

There are allegations that the Ministry of Defence has tried to ignore the issue of Post Traumatic Stress Disorder (PTSD), which left many sufferers emotionally scarred and unable to work, immersed in social dislocation, alcoholism, and depression. Veterans have suffered prolonged personality disorders, flashbacks, and anxiety sometimes reaching pathological levels.

It was revealed that more veterans have committed suicide since the Falklands War ended than the number of servicemen killed in action The South Atlantic Medal Association (SAMA82), which represents and helps Falklands veterans, believes that some 264 veterans had taken their own lives by 2002, a number exceeding the 255 who died in active service, although no estimate is available for the expected number of suicides that would have occurred anyway.

The trials of one British patient, Robert Lawrence, MC, were chronicled in a book co-authored by him entitled *When The Fighting is Over* which was later adapted into a television film. Lawrence was shot at close range by an FN rifle and lost a large percentage of brain matter, but recovered to a degree not thought possible. After the war he became an outspoken critic of the British Army's treatment of Falklands veterans. He remains partially paralysed in the left side of his body.

A similar situation afflicts the veterans on the Argentine side, many of whom have similarly suffered from psychiatric disorders, drug and alcohol abuse, and social turmoil. The current Argentine suicide toll is 454, according to an Argentine film about the suicide of a Falklands veteran.

Source (edited): "http://en.wikipedia.org/wiki/Aftermath_of_the_Falklands_War"

Blatcherism

Blatcherism is a term formed as a portmanteau of the names of two British politicians, Tony Blair (Labour Party) and Margaret Thatcher (Conservative Party). It is used by critics of monetarism and neo-liberal economics to refer to the thesis that a policy model of the Thatcher government, distinct from One Nation Conservatism, was resurrected when Blair came to power. It replaced Butskellism frequently used to describe the post-war consensus on a mixed economy with moderate state intervention to promote social goals, particularly in education and health.

Editorial comment by *Red Pepper* before the 1997 General Election that brought Blair to power may be the earliest usage . Another early sighting of this term was in 2001, used by Brian Lee Crowley, a Canadian commentator. The term has also been used, for example, by the journalist Alexander Cockburn, in preference to Blairism.

Definition

Blatcherism can be defined as an emphasis on free-market policies, support for privatisation or the private ownership of former public services, a monetarist/neo-classical economics economic policy, and a retention of anti-trade union legislation. A convergence of such policies between the Labour and Conservative parties first emerged when Tony Blair became leader of the Labour Party. Blair was elected Leader of the Labour Party in July 1994 following the sudden death of his predecessor, John Smith. Under Blair's leadership the party abandoned many policies it had held for decades and embraced many of the measures enacted by Thatcher led government including the Building Societies (deregulation) Act of 1986. Blair, in conjunction with Peter Mandelson, Gordon Brown and Alastair Campbell, created the New Labour ethos by embracing many aspects of Thatcherite beliefs into Labour as the "Third Way".

The term is also used as shorthand by Ye. V. Ananyeva (*On Modern Ways of Reformism, or On Reformism as Modern Way, Polis Journal* - Political studies - No.5, 2001), according to whom Blatcherism is currently "personified by T. Blair", has "substituted for the previous postwar political consensus", and is "consensual" with "neoconservatism as embodied in thatcherism" in the approach to a solution to Britain's modernisation problems.

According to Richard D. North in "The Politics of Convergence and Divergence", as outcome of the convergences of blatcherism and divergences within blatcherism, in future, in large measure we will be discussing [differences of opinion] in sects, cults, factions and groups... rather than between large parties".

Source (edited): "http://en.wikipedia.org/wiki/Blatcherism"

Bruges Group

The **Bruges Group** is a think tank based in the United Kingdom.

The group is often associated with the Conservative Party, though it is independent of it and remains an all-party organisation. Its Honorary President is Baroness Thatcher, and its Chairman is Barry Legg, who is a businessman and was Chief Executive of the Conservative Party and a former Member of Parliament.

Set up in February 1989, its original aim was to promote the idea of a less centralised European structure than that emerging in Brussels. Its inspiration was Margaret Thatcher's Bruges speech in September 1988, in which she remarked that, "We have not successfully rolled back the frontiers of the state in Britain, only to see them re-imposed at a European level". The Bruges Group's research now includes looking into alternative international relationships for the UK and a complete restructuring of Britain's relationship with other European countries.

Although the Group's President in Baroness Thatcher many senior Labour politicians have addressed their meetings including the former Labour minister Frank Field, MP, Gisela Stuart MP, Lord Stoddart of Swindon and Labour Cabinet Minister the late Rt Hon. Peter Shore.

Bruges Group in the media

Its Director, Robert Oulds, is frequently quoted in the press and makes regular appearances on TV and radio discussing

European issues. Spokesmen for the Bruges Group have also appeared on BBC TV News, ITN; Sky News; The Daily Politics; BBC World Service; BBC R5 Live and international media outlets.

The Bruges Group is also often asked by the media to comment on the particularly vexed issue of the European Union and the Conservative Party.

Activities

The Bruges Group seeks to keep debate on European issues centre stage by commissioning and publishing independent research and by holding meetings and conferences to discuss relevant issues. These seek to inform decision-makers and opinion-formers especially those in Parliament and the media.

As the European Union tries ever more frequently to extend its influence over individual states' right to manage their own affairs, so the Bruges Group has expanded its remit to monitor the EU's policies and regulations relating to the increasing costs of membership, defence, international relations, climate change, national identity, immigration and healthcare.

Internationally the Bruges Group has been particularly active in supporting Euroscepticism in Estonia and discussing issues relating to Turkey and the EU.

The 1980s and 1990s

The group was set up by Lord Harris of High Cross and an Oxford University student Patrick Robertson following Margaret Thatcher's Eurosceptic speech delivered in Bruges in September 1988. It quickly became a focus for Eurosceptic opinion and opposition to the then President of the European Commission, Jacques Delors. The Bruges Group is considered to be the common ancestor of the many British Eurosceptic parties and groups that emerged in the 1990s.

The group was a rallying point for rebellious backbench Conservative MPs during House of Commons debates over the Maastricht Treaty. An Oxford branch was set up (under Roland Smith) with links to Oxford University's growing Eurosceptic movement led by student activist and future Conservative MEP Daniel Hannan. The group then went through a difficult period. Dr Alan Sked, an academic associated with the group, fell out with leading members of the Group during 1991-1992, and went on to form the Anti-Federalist League, which later evolved into the UK Independence Party. Robertson left the group a short time later, later becoming an adviser to Sir James Goldsmith's Referendum Party.

Source (edited): "http://en.wikipedia.org/wiki/Bruges_Group"

Carol Thatcher

Carol Thatcher (born 15 August 1953) is a British journalist, author and media personality. She is the daughter of Margaret Thatcher, Baroness Thatcher, a former British Prime Minister, and Sir Denis Thatcher, Bt.

Thatcher has published biographies of both her parents. Additionally, she produced a documentary of her father which contained his only public interview. Thatcher won the fifth series of the reality show *I'm a Celebrity... Get Me Out of Here!*. In early 2009, she was removed from her on-air position at BBC One after refusing to apologise for making an off-air comment backstage that was deemed a racial pejorative about tennis player Jo-Wilfried Tsonga.

Early life

Carol Thatcher and her twin brother, Sir Mark Thatcher, Bt, were born six weeks prematurely in 1953. According to Margaret Thatcher, Denis Thatcher responded to seeing his offspring for the first time; "My god, they look like rabbits. Put them back." Margaret Thatcher was selected for Finchley in 1958 and was elected as a member of Parliament in 1959. The following year, Thatcher was sent to be educated at Queenswood School, Hertfordshire. Thatcher studied law at University College London before moving to Australia in 1977 to begin a journalism career. While there, her mother was elected Prime Minister. Thatcher has said, "You need quite good shock absorbers and a sense of humour to be the Prime Minister's child."

Career

Thatcher began her journalism career in Australia, working on the *Sydney Morning Herald* from 1977 to 1979. She became a TV reporter at Channel Seven, also in Sydney, and later an interviewer on its morning show. On her return to Britain, she worked as a presenter for LBC, BBC Radio 4, TV-am and wrote travel articles for *The Daily Telegraph*. Due to her mother's high profile political position, many newspapers refused to publish work with her byline.

Thatcher published her first book, *Diary of an election: with Margaret Thatcher on the campaign trail* in 1983. Her second book, a collaboration with tennis player Chris Evert called *Lloyd on Lloyd*, was released three years later. It became Thatcher's first best-seller.

Later publications included a 1996 best-selling biography of her father, *Below the Parapet*. In 2003, Thatcher produced a Channel 4 documentary about him called *Married to Maggie*. Thatcher captured the only public interview Denis Thatcher gave in his lifetime; he died shortly after its release. Thatcher's freelance career has contributed articles to magazines and papers as well as television.

From 2006 to 2009, Thatcher was a freelance contributor to the BBC One magazine programme *The One Show*, making regular filmed reports and joining the presenters and guests in the studio for discussions. On 3 February 2009, British media reported that during the 2009 Australian Open Thatcher had, in a conversation in the show's green room, referred to a black tennis player, reportedly Jo-Wilfried Tsonga, as a golliwog.

According to *The Times*, Thatcher called Tsonga "half-golliwog" and "the golliwog Frog". Presenter Adrian Chiles, comedian Jo Brand, journalists and several guests were with Thatcher when she made the remark. When others protested about her use of the word, Thatcher stated through her spokesperson that the comment was meant in jest.

The BBC stated that Thatcher would not work again on *The One Show* unless she made a more sincere apology. Thatcher refused, saying "I stand by what I said. I wasn't going to apologise. I never meant it in a racist way. It was shorthand. I described someone's appearance colloquially – someone I happen to greatly admire."

Reality Shows

I'm a Celebrity... Get Me Out of Here!

In November 2005 Thatcher was selected to appear with a number of fellow celebrities on the popular ITV television show *I'm a Celebrity... Get Me Out of Here!*. The format of the show meant that she would be forced to spend at least a week in the Australian rainforest with a minimal supply of food in basic living conditions. One of her highlights in the show was for urinating on the ground. She did not own up and the camp accused Sid Owen.

She had to undergo one of the more infamous 'Bushtucker Trials' during her stay in the jungle — which saw her being forced to eat jungle bugs and kangaroo testicles to help sustain her fellow celebrities. Ultimately, she emerged as the fifth series winner and second 'Queen of the Jungle'.

100% English

DNA tests in association with a reality TV programme *100% English* screened on Channel 4 on 13 November 2006 indicate that Thatcher may be descended from a Bedouin tribe, or that her origins may date to the desert farmers of ancient Mesopotamia, which centuries ago covered all of Iraq and large portions of contemporary Turkey, Syria and Iran.

Most Haunted

Thatcher appeared on LIVINGtv show *Most Haunted* on 13 February 2007 as a celebrity guest alongside presenter Yvette Fielding and Medium David Wells to search for paranormal activity at Tatton Hall in Cheshire.

Mummy's War

In 2007, Carol Thatcher travelled to the Falkland Islands and Argentina for the documentary *Mummy's War*, in order to explore the legacy of the Falklands War. Whilst receiving a highly positive reception from the pro-British islanders (who regard her mother as a heroine), her reception in Argentina provoked protests and demonstrations (including the cry "your mother is a war criminal!"). During her stay in Argentina she met a group of mothers who lost their sons during the conflict and stated, "We were fighting a war; we won, you lost" and reminding them that it was their country that invaded the islands, thus initiating the conflict. The interview ended with one of the women claiming that "God will punish her [Margaret Thatcher]".

Source (edited): "http://en.wikipedia.org/wiki/Carol_Thatcher"

Centre for Policy Studies

The **Centre for Policy Studies (CPS)** is a British Conservative policy studies think tank whose goal is to promote coherent and practical public policy, to roll back the state, reform public services, support communities, and challenge threats to Britain's independence.

It was founded by Conservatives Sir Keith Joseph and Margaret Thatcher in 1974 to champion economic liberalism in Britain and has since played a global role in the dissemination of free market economics along monetarist and, what today would be called, neoliberal lines. Its policy proposals are claimed to be based on the principles of individual choice and responsibility. They also assert that they prioritise the concepts of duty, family, liberty, and the rule of law. The CPS has a stated goal of serving as the champion of the small state.

The CPS soon drove for a reassessment of Conservative economic policy during their period in opposition from 1974-1979. It was during this period that the CPS released its landmark reports, such as *Stranded on the Middle Ground* and *Monetarism is Not Enough* (1974 and 1976). Keith Joseph's keynote speeches, published by the CPS, aimed to lead the way in changing the climate of opinion in Britain and set the intellectual foundations for the free market reforms of the 1980s. Monetarism is Not Enough was described by Margaret Thatcher as "one of the very few speeches which have fundamentally affected a political generation's way of thinking.".

The CPS did not consciously represent itself as a partisan institute; 'blame' for the collectivist post-war consensus was placed on both sides of the political parties for operating within the same ideological framework. The CPS continually advocated a centre-right approach and was hugely influential during Margaret Thatcher's administration, operating as a key driving force towards her hallmark policies of privatization, deregulation and monetarism

In her own words, its job was to 'expose the follies and self-defeating consequences of government intervention....'to think the unthinkable'. In 1982, it released *Telecommunications in Britain*, which urged the Government to embrace a fuller agenda of privatization in the telecoms sector. The paper recommended the privatization of British Telecom and the introduction of competition to the sector –both of which were implemented. Another key publication was *The Performance of the Privatised Industries* (1996) – a four volume statistical analysis which showed how the privatization agenda had benefitted the consumer by ushering in lower prices and higher quality service. It argued that the taxpayer had benefitted greatly from privatisation - not just from the initial windfall from receipts, but also from higher tax revenues than had ever been received from the same companies when they were in state ownership.

Recent history

More recently, the CPS has focused on the area of social policy, for example *The Price of Parenthood* (Jill Kirby, 2005), a study which claimed to show how the state both penalizes marriage and subsidises family breakup. Its call for marriage to be recognized in the tax system is now official Conservative Party policy.

In 2009, the CPS celebrated its 35th Anniversary for which the Leader of the Opposition, David Cameron MP, gave a speech highlighting the role the CPS played in the Conservative Party's victory in the 1979 election crediting them with 'a great rebirth of intellectual ideas, of intellectual vigour, and of intellectual leadership'

People
- Chairman: Lord Saatchi
- Acting Director: Tim Knox
- Deputy Director of Events and Funding: Jenny Nicholson
- Research Economist: Ryan Bourne
- Executive Assistant: Kate Jones

Policies

Economy - The CPS 'believes in regulation that does not inhibit the growth of business, taxes that do not act as a disincentive to work or to investment in the UK, and a leaner more effective state that avoids unnecessary intervention in the economy'.

Family – The CPS advocates that fiscal policy should be reformed to support marriage through the tax system and to remove the welfare penalty on two-parent families. State intervention in family life should focus on protection of vulnerable children; it should not extend to managing their day-to-day lives and removing responsibility and judgment from parents.

Energy - Recent CPS publications have argued that the UK must develop its nuclear, clean coal (including coal gasification) and efficient renewable supplies of energy.

Public Services - The CPS has been a consistent advocate for greater choice and diversity of provision, opening up state monopolies to new providers and putting greater power and responsibility in the hands of parents and patients.

Drugs - The CPS' Prison and Addiction forum (PANDA) was set up in 2008. It provides an independent forum of debate about drugs policy for academics, practitioners, psychiatrists, and specialist commentators. Its aim is to identify the reforms required in the UK to get our drug problem under control, to prevent drug use and to offer substance abusers the help and necessary care to combat their abuse.

Broadcasting – The CPS believes that public intervention should be focussed on where there is genuine 'market failure' and the remit and funding of the BBC should reflect this.

Recent Publications
- *A Magna Carta for Localism*
- *An End to Factory Schools*
- *Be Bold for Growth*
- *More Bang for the Buck*
- *A Step Change in UK Philanthropy*

Source (edited): "http://en.wikipedia.org/wiki/Centre_for_Policy_Studies"

Conservative Party (UK) leadership election, 1975

Edward Heath, leader of the Conservative Party and Prime Minister of the United Kingdom had called and unexpectedly lost the February 1974 general election. Although the Labour Party were able only to form a minority government, the following October 1974 general election saw them obtain a small majority.

At the time the rules for electing a party leader only applied when the post was vacant and there was no way to challenge an incumbent. Heath faced many critics calling for either his resignation and/or a change in the rules for leadership elections to allow for a challenge. Heath eventually agreed with the 1922 Committee that there would be a review of the rules for leadership elections and subsequently he would put himself up for re-election.

A review was conducted under the auspices of Heath's predecessor Sir Alec Douglas-Home. Two recommendations were made, though neither was to make a difference in 1975 (although they would prove crucial in future years). The leader would henceforth be elected annually, whether the party was in opposition or government, in the period following a Queen's Speech, though in most years this would prove a formality. Also on the first round the requirement for a victorious candidate to have a lead of 15% over their nearest rival was modified so that this would now be 15% of the total number of MPs, not just those voting for candidates.

Following the review, Heath called a leadership election for 4 February 1975, in order to assert his authority as leader of the party. Many expected the contest to be a walkover, believing there was no clear alternative to Heath after Keith Joseph had ruled himself out following controversial remarks and William Whitelaw had pledged loyalty to Heath. However Margaret Thatcher opted to stand, as did the fringe backbencher Hugh Fraser. Even then many believed that Heath would win easily. Thatcher's support was seen as minimal, with all the Conservative supporting daily newspapers backing Heath (although the weekly *The Spectator* backed Thatcher).

The first ballot had the following result:

Heath resigned, but another ballot was needed. This was held on 11 February. Thatcher was the first (and to date the only) woman to be elected leader of a major political party in the United Kingdom. (Margaret Beckett was leader of the Labour Party from John Smith's death in May 1994 until the election of

Tony Blair in July 1994, and Harriet Harman served as acting Labour leader from Gordon Brown's resignation in May 2010 until September 2010, but neither Beckett nor Harman was elected to such a position.)

Source (edited): "http://en.wikipedia.org/wiki/Conservative_Party_(UK)_leadership_election,_1975"

Conservative Party (UK) leadership election, 1989

The **1989 Conservative Party leadership election** took place on 5 December 1989. The incumbent Margaret Thatcher was opposed by the little known 69-year-old backbencher MP Sir Anthony Meyer, Bt.

Background

During 1989 the Conservative government led by Thatcher had run into difficulties. The Chancellor of the Exchequer, Nigel Lawson, had resigned in October over Thatcher's determination to to follow the advice of her advisers, specifically Sir Alan Walters. In 1989 Labour won their first national electoral victory since 1974 in the elections to the European Parliament, beating the Conservatives. Opinion polls were also starting to show a Labour lead.

As a result Thatcher faced mounting internal party criticism, which culminated in the decision of Meyer to offer a stalking horse candidacy for the party leadership.

Sir Anthony Meyer was critical of the Community Charge, Thatcher's leadership style and her Euroscepticism.

Thatcher won the contest overwhelmingly and her campaign was organised by former UK Cabinet minister, George Younger. She announced to the press outside 10 Downing Street, Thatcher said:

I would like to say how very pleased I am with this result and how very pleased I am to have had the overwhelming support of my colleagues in the House and the people from the party in the country.

However, a total of 60 Conservative MPs failed to support Thatcher by either actively voting for Meyer, spoiling their ballot papers, or abstaining. After the ballot Meyer said:

I was quite surprised to get so many votes, I thought I'd be beaten by the abstentions. The total result I think is rather better than I'd expected and not quite as good as some of my friends were hoping for.

Within the year, as Poll tax sparked public uproar, the economy slid towards recession and the Labour lead in the opinion polls mounted into double digits, Thatcher would be ousted as party leader and Prime Minister of the United Kingdom following a further contest in November 1990.

Source (edited): "http://en.wikipedia.org/wiki/Conservative_Party_(UK)_leadership_election,_1989"

Conservative Party (UK) leadership election, 1990

The **1990 Conservative Party leadership election** in the United Kingdom took place in November 1990 following the decision of former Defence and Environment Secretary Michael Heseltine to stand against the incumbent Conservative leader and Prime Minister, Margaret Thatcher.

Thatcher failed to win outright under the terms of the election in the first ballot, and was persuaded to withdraw from the second round of voting. This marked the end of her eleven-year premiership and resulted in the election of John Major, then Chancellor of the Exchequer, as her successor.

Background to the contest

Discontent with Thatcher's leadership of the party had been growing over the latter years of her tenure. In December 1989, she had been challenged for the leadership for the first time since her election in 1975, by the backbench MP Sir Anthony Meyer. Thatcher faced no serious threat of losing to this stalking horse challenger, but her political impregnability was undermined by the fact that sixty MPs had not voted for her.

Throughout 1990, Thatcher's popularity — and that of the Conservative government — waned considerably. Whereas in 1987 Thatcher had presided over an economic boom, by 1989-90 interest rates had to be hiked to 15% to cool inflation which was now in double digits - and by late 1990 the economy was in recession. The introduction of the deeply unpopular Community Charge (labelled 'Poll Tax') had been greeted with widespread non-payment and even a riot in Trafalgar Square in April 1990. Labour held a lead in most of the opinion polls since mid 1989 and at the height of the Poll tax controversy, one opinion poll had shown Labour support in excess of 50% with a lead of more than 20 points over the Tories.

There were differences within the Cabinet over Thatcher's perceived intransigence in her approach to the European Economic Community — in particular many leading Conservatives wanted Britain to join the Exchange Rate Mechanism, a move which Thatcher did not favour. In 1989 the then Foreign Secretary Sir Geoffrey Howe and Chancellor Nigel Lawson forced Thatcher to agree to the "Madrid Conditions", namely that Britain would eventually join the ERM "when the time was right". In July 1989 she retaliated by removing Howe from the Foreign Office, moving him to Deputy Prime Minister. Lawson - who had clashed with Thatcher over "shadowing the Deutschmark" early in 1988 - then resigned as Chancellor in October 1989, unable to accept Thatcher taking independent advice from the economist Alan Walters. The beneficiary of these moves was the hitherto-unknown Chief

Secretary to the Treasury, John Major, who briefly succeeded Howe as Foreign Secretary before succeeding Lawson as Chancellor, putting him in pole position to succeed Thatcher. In October 1990 Major and Foreign Secretary Douglas Hurd finally obtained agreement from a reluctant Thatcher that Britain should join the ERM.

In her Party Conference Speech early in October, Thatcher mocked the Liberal Democrats' new "bird" logo in language lifted from the famous "Monty Python" "Dead Parrot" sketch. This looked more than slightly foolish when the Liberal Democrats captured a seat off the Conservatives at the Eastbourne by-election (caused by the assassination of Ian Gow by the IRA at the end of July) on 18 October.

The event normally seen as the 'final straw' in the run-up to the contest is the resignation of the Deputy Prime Minister, Sir Geoffrey Howe, on 1 November. This was a response to comments by Thatcher in the House of Commons on 31 October, when she criticised the vision of European integration, including a Single Currency, espoused by the European Commission under Jacques Delors, characterising it as the path to a federal European superstate, and famously declared that her response to such a vision would be "No. No. No" (In June 1990 Chancellor Major had suggested that the proposed Single European Currency should be a "hard ecu", competing for use against existing national currencies; this idea was not in the end adopted).

Howe did not make his resignation speech immediately because he had temporarily lost his voice. At the Lord Mayor's Banquet on 12 November Thatcher dismissed Howe's resignation by employing a cricketing metaphor:
I am still at the crease, though the bowling has been pretty hostile of late. And in case anyone doubted it, can I assure you there will be no ducking the bouncers, no stonewalling, no playing for time. The bowling's going to get hit all round the ground. That is my style.
The next day, Howe made his resignation speech from the backbenches, addressing his dismay at her approach and, famously responding to Thatcher's cricketing metaphor by employing one of his own. Explaining how, in his opinion, her approach made it hard for British ministers to negotiate for Britain's interests in Europe he declared:
It is rather like sending your opening batsmen to the crease only for them to find, the moment the first balls are bowled, that their bats have been broken before the game by the team captain.
Howe reinforced the change in general perception of Thatcher from the 'Iron Lady' to a divisive and confrontational figure. Within a week, another critic, former minister Michael Heseltine, had announced that he would challenge her for the leadership of the party.

Contest rules

Under the rules at the time, introduced in 1965 and modified in 1975, there would be a series of ballots, conducted by the 1922 Committee, with that committee's chairman, Cranley Onslow, serving as Returning Officer.

In the first round a candidate needed to win the backing of an absolute majority of MPs. In addition they needed to have a margin over their nearest rival of 15% of the total electorate. This latter rule had been modified from 15% of those voting in the 1975 review and was to prove a crucial distinction in the 1990 contest when Margaret Thatcher narrowly missed this new target.

If neither candidate achieved a sufficiently large majority, then a second ballot would take place the following week. Nominations would be re-opened, and at this stage an absolute majority only would be required. If this did not happen, then the top three candidates would go forward to a third round which would be held using the alternative vote system.

Because of this process, the first round was widely regarded as the real test of confidence in Thatcher. Many speculated that, if she did not achieve outright victory, then she would either be forced to step down and open up the field to others or else suffer further challenges from heavyweight figures in the party. Although Heseltine was known to be a serious contender for the leadership in his own right, many saw him also fulfilling the role of a "stalking horse" to push Thatcher out and pave the way for victory by a third candidate in a later round.

First ballot

The first ballot in the election took place on Tuesday 20 November 1990. Thatcher herself was at the Fontainebleau European summit on the night of the contest and therefore voted by proxy, perhaps anticipating a better result than she actually achieved.

Although receiving the support of a clear majority of MPs, Thatcher narrowly failed to achieve a lead over Heseltine that comprised at least 15% of the number of all Conservative MPs, abstentions and spoilt ballots included. (Had the contest been run on the pre 1975 rules, she would have won outright at this stage.) The contest therefore had to move into a second ballot. Thatcher gave a short statement in Paris following the announcement of the result, declaring that she intended to contest the second ballot, and on her return to London declared "I fight on; I fight to win."

Hurd and Major pledged their support, as did Cecil Parkinson, Kenneth Baker and ex-Cabinet minister Nicholas Ridley. Norman Tebbit, another ex-Cabinet minister, was part of her campaign team, along with John Wakeham. Thatcher's campaign manager, Peter Morrison, advised her to consult Cabinet members one by one. Cabinet ministers had decided before consulting Thatcher the line they would each take: though they personally would support her in the second ballot, they thought that she would lose. Peter Lilley, William Waldegrave, John Gummer and Chris Patten stuck to this line. Kenneth Clarke, the Secretary of State for Education, famously became the first of her ministers to advise her that she could not win but that he would support her as Prime Minister for another five or ten years. Malcolm Rifkind said she would not win and was unsure whether he could support her in the second ballot. Peter Brooke said he would support Thatcher whatever she chose to do and that she could win "with all guns blazing". Michael Howard doubted whether she could win but said he would campaign full-heartedly for her.

Thatcher therefore decided to withdraw her candidacy on Thursday 22 November 1990. As a result of this, two further candidates allowed themselves to be nominated: the Foreign Secretary Douglas Hurd and the Chancellor of the Exchequer John Major.

The second round of voting took place on Tuesday 27 November 1990. Major, seen as relatively new blood in the government, secured a commanding lead - although with fewer votes than Thatcher had obtained in the first ballot - of 185 votes to Michael Heseltine's 131 votes and Douglas Hurd's 56. Even so, this was technically a few votes short of a clear victory and a third round would have been held on Thursday 29 November 1990. However, within minutes of the result, Heseltine and Hurd withdrew from the contest in Major's favour. It was therefore announced by the Chairman of the 1922 Committee, Cranley Onslow, that no third round would be necessary, and that Major was elected unopposed.

Reaction

The Sun newspaper, a firm supporter of Thatcher and her party since her election campaign in 1979, marked her resignation with the front page headline "MRS T-EARS" - in reference to her breaking down in tears after announcing her resignation.

Labour opposition leader Neil Kinnock (whose party had been ascendant in the opinion polls since the announcement of the Poll tax more than a year earlier) described Mrs Thatcher's resignation as "very good news" and demanded an immediate general election.

Outcome

John Major was declared the leader of the party on the evening of Tuesday 27 November 1990. Following Thatcher's formal resignation, HM The Queen invited Major to kiss hands the next day. Douglas Hurd was re-appointed as Foreign Secretary and Michael Heseltine returned to the Cabinet as Environment Secretary, a post he had held in the early 1980s. Both Hurd and Heseltine remained key figures during the Major government, Heseltine eventually rising to become Deputy Prime Minister in 1995.

Major's premiership began well, and he was credited with restoring a consensual style of Cabinet government after the years of forceful leadership under Margaret Thatcher. The First Gulf War in early 1991 contributed to strong public support. He secured some foreign policy successes in Europe, negotiating the Maastricht Treaty after securing an opt-out from the Social Chapter and the single currency, and he sprung a surprise victory in the 1992 election, securing a majority of 21 while polling more votes than any other party in British electoral history.

Nevertheless the political tides soon turned. The government's reputation for economic competence was destroyed by Britain's ejection from the Exchange Rate Mechanism in September 1992, leading to inevitable protests e.g. from Norman Tebbit at the 1992 Party Conference, that the Conservatives had been wrong to ignore Thatcher's wishes to stay out (whether Britain entered the ERM at too high an exchange rate has been a source of debate ever since). Apart from a brief period during the fuel protests in 2000 the Conservatives would not again enjoy an opinion poll lead until after the election of David Cameron as leader in 2005. The ongoing rebellion in the first half of 1993 by Conservative backbenchers against the passage of the Maastricht Treaty through the House of Commons was also deeply damaging to the government. Many of the Maastricht rebels were Thatcher supporters, and one of them, Teresa Gorman, devoted the opening chapter of her memoir of the incident to an account of the 1990 leadership contest. The massive Conservative defeat in 1997 was thus attributable, at least in part, to the perception of internal division over Europe which had first been exposed by the 1990 leadership election.

Source (edited): "http://en.wikipedia.org/wiki/Conservative_Party_(UK)_leadership_election,_1990"

Denis Thatcher

Major **Sir Denis Thatcher, 1st Baronet**, MBE, TD (10 May 1915 – 26 June 2003) was a British businessman, and the husband of the former British Prime Minister, Margaret Thatcher. He was born in Lewisham, London, the elder child of a New Zealand-born British businessman, Thomas Herbert (Jack) Thatcher, and his wife (Lilian) Kathleen, *née* Bird. He is the most recent person outside the Royal Family to be awarded a hereditary title.

Early life

At the age of eight he entered a preparatory school as a boarder in Bognor Regis, following which he attended the nonconformist public school, Mill Hill. At school he excelled at cricket, being a left-handed batsman. Thatcher left Mill Hill at the age of 18 to join the family paint and preservatives business, Atlas Preservatives. He enlisted in the army shortly after the Munich crisis, as he was convinced war was imminent. This was reinforced by a visit he made to Germany with his father's business in 1938.

War record

During the Second World War, he initially served in the 34th Searchlight (Queen's Own Royal West Kent Regiment) of the Royal Engineers as a second lieutenant. He transferred to the Royal Artillery on 1 August 1940. During the war he was promoted to war substantive captain and temporary major. Although, to his regret, he saw no real fighting—despite serving through the Invasion of Sicily and the Italian Campaign—he was twice Mentioned in Despatches, and in 1945 was appointed a Member of the Order of the British Empire (MBE). The first Mention came on 11 January 1945, for service in Italy, and the second on 29 November 1945, again for Italian service. His MBE was gazetted on 20 September 1945, and was for his efforts in initiating and supporting Operation Goldflake, the transfer of I Canadian Corps from Italy to the North-West European theatre of operations. By this time Thatcher was based in Marseilles, attached to HQ 203 sub-area. In the recommendation for the MBE (dated 28 March 1945), his commanding officer wrote "Maj. THATCHER set an outstanding example of energy, initiative and drive. He deserves most of the credit for [...] the excellence of the work done." He also received the French approximate equivalent of a Mention when he was cited in orders at Corps d'Armée level for his efforts in promoting smooth relations between the Commonwealth military forces and the French civil and military authorities. He was promoted to substantive lieutenant on 11 April 1945. Demobilised in 1946, he returned to run the family business, his father having died, aged 57, on 24 June 1943, when Thatcher was in Sicily. Due to army commitments, Thatcher did not attend the funeral.

He remained in the Territorial Army reserve of officers until reaching the age limit for service on 10 May 1965, when he retired, retaining the honorary rank of major. He was awarded the Territorial Efficiency Decoration (TD) for his service on 21 September 1982.

Marriages

On 28 March 1942, Thatcher married Margaret Doris Kempson, (23 January 1918 - 8 June 1996), the daughter of Leonard Kempson, a businessman at St. Mary's Church, Monken Hadley. They had met at an officer's dance at Grosvenor House the year before.

Although initially very happy, Thatcher and his first wife never lived together. Their married life became confined to snatched weekends and irregular leaves as Thatcher was often abroad during the war. When Thatcher returned to England after being demobilised in 1946, his wife told him she had met someone else and wanted a divorce. Their childless marriage ended in the first weeks of 1948. Kempson married Sir (Alfred) Howard Whitby Hickman, 3rd Baronet (1920-1979) on 24 January the same year. Thatcher was so traumatised by the event that he refused fully to talk about his first marriage or the separation, even to his daughter, as she states in her 1995 biography of him. Thatcher's two children only found out about his first marriage in February 1976 by chance, when the media revealed it.

In February 1949, while attending a Paint Trades Federation function in Dartford, he met Margaret Roberts, a chemist and newly-selected parliamentary candidate. They married on 13 December 1951, at Wesley's Chapel in City Road, London. This was because Methodism was also Margaret Roberts's religion, but also because as a divorced man, Thatcher could not at the time remarry in an Anglican church.

They later had twin children, Carol and Mark, who were born on 15 August 1953.

Career

Thatcher financed his wife's training as a barrister and a home in Chelsea; he also bought a large house in Lamberhurst, Kent in 1965. His firm employed 200 people by 1957, but he sold it to Castrol on 26 August 1965 after suffering a mild nervous breakdown in 1964. He received a seat on Castrol's parent board, which he maintained when Burmah Oil took it over in 1966. He retired from Burmah in June 1975, four months after his wife won the Conservative Party leadership election.

In addition to being a director of Burmah, he was chairman of the Atlas Preservative Co, vice-chairman of Attwoods plc from 1983 to January 1994, a director of Quinton Hazell plc from 1968 to 1998 and a consultant to Amec plc and CSX Corp. He was also a non-executive director of Halfords in the mid-1980s.

Public life and perceptions

In an interview with Kirsten Cubitt in early October 1970, Thatcher said, "I don't pretend that I'm anything but an honest-to-God right-winger - those are my views and I don't care who knows 'em."

Thatcher agreed with his wife on most political issues, though he was strongly against the death penalty, calling it "absolutely awful" and "barbaric", while she favoured it. Thatcher was anti-socialist. He told his daughter in 1995 that he would have banned Trade Unions altogether in Britain. Thatcher hated the BBC, thinking it was biased against the Thatcher government, as well as unpatriotic. In his most famous outburst about the BBC, he claimed his wife had been "stitched up by bloody BBC poofs and Trots" when she was questioned by a member of the public about the sinking of the ARA General Belgrano on *Nationwide* in 1983.

The public perception of his character was formed to an extent by a series of spoof letters published in the satirical magazine *Private Eye* in the 1980s. The "Dear Bill" column written by Richard Ingrams and John Wells after May 1979 took the form of a letter purported to be from Denis to his real life friend and golfing partner Bill Deedes (former editor of *The Daily Telegraph*), detailing life at Number 10. The letters portrayed Denis Thatcher as a reactionary interested only in golf and gin. John Wells used the character portrayed in the letters, and created the stage play *Anyone for Denis* (also shown on television). Thatcher started to play along — Ulster Unionist David Burnside recalled a reception in Blackpool "to which Sir Denis came along with his minder and declared: 'I don't know what reception I'm at, but for God's sake give me a gin and tonic'".

Thatcher refused press interviews and only made brief speeches. When he did speak to the press, he called Margaret "The Boss". One lapse, which he regretted for the ensuing controversy he felt was at his wife's expense, was in December 1979, when at a dinner of the London Society of Rugby Football Union Referees (of which he was treasurer, having refereed at a club level for many years) he made remarks criticising the sporting boycott of South Africa. Thatcher said, "We are a free people, playing an amateur game, and sure as hell we have the right to tour South Africa".

He was known as an irreverent, good-natured man with a talent for friendship. Margaret Thatcher often acknowledged her husband's support. In her autobiography she wrote: "I could never have been Prime Minister for more than 11 years without Denis by my side." He saw his role as helping her survive the stress of the job, which he urged her to resign on the 10th anniversary of her becoming Prime Minister, in 1989, sensing that otherwise she would be forced out (as happened a year later). After his wife's third election victory in 1987, whilst watching his wife wave to the cheering crowds outside Downing Street, Thatcher said quietly to his daughter Carol, "In a year's time she will be so unpopular you won't believe it". In fact, this happened 12–18 months later than when he predicted, but was still accurate.

In December 1990, it was announced that Denis Thatcher would be created a baronet (the first since 1964). The award was gazetted in February 1991 as Sir Denis Thatcher, 1st Baronet, of Scotney in the County of Kent. This meant that his wife was entitled to be called Lady Thatcher whilst retaining her seat in the House of Commons, and was also a hereditary title that was to be inherited by their son Mark after Denis's death. It was the last British hereditary honour to be granted to anyone outside the royal family. However, Sir Denis Thatcher's wife was created a life peeress as Baroness Thatcher in her own right in 1992 after her retirement from the House of Commons. He and his wife were one of the few married couples who both hold titles in their own right.

Death

On 17 January 2003, Sir Denis Thatcher underwent a six-hour heart bypass operation. He had been complaining of breathlessness in the weeks before Christmas 2002 and the problem was spotted in early January. He left the hospital on 28 January 2003, and appeared to have made a full recovery. He visited his son Mark in South Africa in April but by the middle of June he complained of breathlessness once again. He was taken to hospital where pancreatic cancer was diagnosed, along with fluid in his lungs. He died of pancreatic cancer on 26 June at the age of 88 at Westminster's Lister Hospital in London. His funeral service was held on 3 July 2003, at the chapel of the Royal Hospital in Chelsea, after which his body was cremated at Mortlake Crematorium in Richmond, London. On 30 October his memorial service was held in Westminster Abbey.

Source (edited): "http://en.wikipedia.org/wiki/Denis_Thatcher"

Electoral history of Margaret Thatcher

This is a summary of the **electoral history of Margaret Thatcher**, who was Prime Minister of the United Kingdom from 1979 to 1990 and leader of the Conservative Party from 1975 to 1990.

She was the Member of Parliament (MP) for Finchley from 1959 to 1992.

Parliamentary Elections

1950 General Election, Dartford

1951 General Election, Dartford

1959 General Election, Finchley

1964 General Election, Finchley

1966 General Election, Finchley

1970 General Election, Finchley

February 1974 General Election, Finchley

October 1974 General Election, Finchley

1979 General Election, Finchley

1983 General Election, Finchley

1987 General Election, Finchley

Heath resigned as Conservative leader, but another ballot was needed. This was held on 11 February.

Although receiving the support of a clear majority of MPs, Thatcher narrowly failed to achieve a lead over Heseltine that comprised at least 15% of the number of all Conservative MPs, abstentions and spoilt ballots included. Thatcher therefore decided to withdraw her candidacy on Thursday 22 November 1990. As a result of this, two further candidates allowed themselves to be nominated: the Foreign Secretary Douglas Hurd and the Chancellor of the Exchequer John Major. John Major subsequently won the leadership election and was made Prime Minister.
All parties shown.
All parties with more than 500 votes shown.
All parties gaining over 500 votes listed.
Source (edited): "http://en.wikipedia.org/wiki/Electoral_history_of_Margaret_Thatcher"

Falklands War

The **Falklands War** (Spanish: *Guerra de las Malvinas/Guerra del Atlántico Sur*), also called the **Falklands Conflict/Crisis**, was fought in 1982 between Argentina and the United Kingdom (UK) over the disputed Falkland Islands and South Georgia and the South Sandwich Islands. The Falkland Islands consist of two large and many small islands in the South Atlantic Ocean east of Argentina; their name and sovereignty over them is disputed.

The Falklands War started on Friday, 2 April 1982, with the Argentine invasion and occupation of the Falkland Islands and South Georgia. Britain launched a naval task force to engage the Argentine Navy and Argentine Air Force, and retake the islands by amphibious assault. The conflict ended with the Argentine surrender on 14 June 1982, and the islands remained under British control. The war lasted 74 days. It resulted in the deaths of 257 British and 649 Argentine soldiers, sailors, and airmen, and the deaths of three civilian Falkland Islanders. It is the most recent external conflict to be fought by the UK without any allied states and the only external Argentine war since the 1880s.

The conflict was the result of a protracted historical confrontation regarding the sovereignty of the islands. Neither state officially declared war and the fighting was largely limited to the territories under dispute and the South Atlantic. The initial invasion was characterised by Argentina as the re-occupation of its own territory, and by the UK as an invasion of a British dependent territory. As of 2011, and as it has since the 19th century, Argentina shows no sign of relinquishing its claim. The claim remained in the Argentine constitution after its reformation in 1994.

The political effects of the war were strong in both countries. A wave of patriotic sentiment swept through both: the Argentine loss prompted even larger protests against the ruling military government, which hastened its downfall; in the United Kingdom, the government of Prime Minister Margaret Thatcher was bolstered. It helped Thatcher's government to victory in the 1983 general election, which prior to the war was seen as by no means certain. The war has played an important role in the culture of both countries, and has been the subject of several books, films, and songs. Over time, the cultural and political weight of the conflict has had less effect on the British public than on that of Argentina, where the war is still a topic of discussion.

Relations between Argentina and UK were restored in 1989 under the *umbrella formula* which states that the islands' sovereignty dispute would remain aside.

Lead-up to the conflict

In the period leading up to the war, and especially following the transfer of power between military dictators General Jorge Rafael Videla and General Roberto Eduardo Viola in late-March 1981, Argentina had been in the midst of a devastating economic crisis and large-scale civil unrest against the military *junta* that had been governing the country since 1976. In December 1981 there was a further change in the Argentine military regime bringing to office a new *junta* headed by General Leopoldo Galtieri (acting president), Brigadier Basilio Lami Dozo and Admiral Jorge Anaya. Anaya was the main architect and supporter of a military solution for the long standing claim over the islands, calculating that the United Kingdom would never respond militarily. In doing so the Galtieri government hoped to mobilise Argentines' long-standing patriotic feelings towards the islands and thus divert public attention from the country's chronic economic problems and the regime's ongoing human rights violations. Such action would also bolster its dwindling legitimacy. The newspaper *La Prensa* speculated in a step-by-step plan beginning with cutting off supplies to the Islands, ending in direct actions late 1982, if the UN talks were fruitless.

Admiral Jorge Anaya was the driving force in the Junta's decision to invade.

The ongoing tension between the two countries over the islands increased on 19 March when a group of hired Argentine scrap metal merchants raised the Argentine flag at South Georgia, an act that would later be seen as the first offensive action in the war. The Argentine military junta, suspecting that the UK would reinforce its South Atlantic

Forces, ordered the invasion of the Falkland Islands to be brought forward to 2 April.

Britain was initially taken by surprise by the Argentine attack on the South Atlantic islands, despite repeated warnings by Royal Navy captain Nicholas Barker and others. Barker believed that the intention expressed in Defence Secretary John Nott's 1981 review to withdraw the Royal Navy ship HMS *Endurance*, Britain's only naval presence in the South Atlantic, sent a signal to the Argentines that Britain was unwilling, and would soon be unable, to defend its territories and subjects in the Falklands.

War

Invasion by Argentina

On 2 April 1982, Argentine forces mounted amphibious landings of the Falkland Islands, following the civilian occupation of South Georgia on 19 March, before the Falklands War began. The invasion met a nominal defence organised by the Falkland Islands' Governor Sir Rex Hunt giving command to Major Mike Norman of the Royal Marines, the landing of Lieutenant Commander Guillermo Sanchez-Sabarots' Amphibious Commandos Group, the attack on Moody Brook barracks, the engagement between the troops of Hugo Santillan and Bill Trollope at Stanley, and the final engagement and surrender at Government House.

Initial British response to the invasion

HMS *Invincible*, part of the task force.

Word of the invasion apparently first reached Britain via amateur radio.

The retaking of the Falkland Islands was considered extremely difficult: the main constraint was the disparity in deployable air cover. The British had 34 Harrier aircraft against approximately 122 servicable jet fighters, of which about 50 were employed as air superiority fighters and the remainder as strike aircraft, in Argentina's air forces during the war. The U.S. Navy considered a successful counter-invasion by the British to be 'a military impossibility'.

The United States initially tried to mediate an end to the conflict. However, when Argentina refused the U.S. peace overtures, U.S. Secretary of State Alexander Haig announced that the United States would prohibit arms sales to Argentina and provide material support for British operations. Both Houses of the U.S. Congress passed resolutions supporting the U.S. action siding with the United Kingdom.

By mid-April, the Royal Air Force had set up an airbase at Wideawake on the mid-Atlantic British overseas territory of Ascension Island, including a sizeable force of Avro Vulcan B Mk 2 bombers, Handley Page Victor K Mk 2 refuelling aircraft, and McDonnell Douglas Phantom FGR Mk 2 fighters to protect them. Meanwhile the main British naval task force arrived at Ascension to prepare for active service. A small force had already been sent south to recapture South Georgia.

Encounters began in April; the British Task Force was shadowed by Boeing 707 aircraft of the Argentine Air Force during their travel to the south. Several of these flights were intercepted by BAE Sea Harriers outside the British-imposed exclusion zone; the unarmed 707s were not attacked because diplomatic moves were still in progress and the UK had not yet decided to commit itself to armed force. On 23 April a Brazilian commercial Douglas DC-10 from VARIG Airlines en route to South Africa was intercepted by British Harriers who visually identified the civilian plane.

Position of third party countries

The USA provided political support voting for UN resolution 502 requesting the departure of Argentine troops. They also discreetly provided the United Kingdom with military equipment ranging from submarine detectors to the latest missiles.

France provided political support, voting for UN resolution 502. The French also provided dissimilar aircraft training allowing Harrier pilots to train against French aircraft used by Argentina. French and British intelligence also worked to prevent Argentina from obtaining more Exocets on the international market.

New Zealand sent a frigate to relieve a British ship in the Indian Ocean, thus assisting the Royal Navy to meet its commitments in the South Atlantic.

Chile gave support to Britain in the form of Intelligence about Argentine military and radar early warning.

On the Argentine side, Peru and Venezuela sent aircraft spare parts, Brazil leased two P-95 maritime patrol aircraft and Israeli IAI advisors already in the country continued their work during the conflict. . The Soviet Union provided intelligence on British military movements, and facilitated the supply by Libya of strela 2 missiles.

Recapture of South Georgia and the attack on the *Santa Fe*

The scope of the conflict

The South Georgia force, *Operation Paraquet*, under the command of Major Guy Sheridan RM, consisted of Marines from 42 Commando, a troop of the Special Air Service (SAS) and Special Boat Service (SBS) troops who were intended to land as reconnaissance forces for an invasion by the Royal Marines. All were embarked on *RFA Tidespring*. First to arrive was the *Churchill*-class submarine HMS *Conqueror* on 19 April, and the island was over-flown by a radar-mapping Handley Page Victor on 20 April.

The first landings of SAS troops took place on 21 April, but—with the southern hemisphere autumn setting in—the weather was so bad that their landings and others made the next day were all withdrawn after two helicopters crashed in fog on Fortuna Glacier. On 23 April, a submarine alert was sounded and operations were halted, with the *Tidespring* being withdrawn to deeper water to avoid interception. On 24 April, the British forces regrouped and headed in to attack.

On 25 April, after resupplying the Argentine garrison in South Georgia, the submarine ARA *Santa Fe* was spotted on the surface by a Westland Wessex HAS Mk 3 helicopter from HMS *Antrim*, which attacked the Argentine submarine with depth charges. HMS *Plymouth* launched a Westland Wasp HAS.Mk.1 helicopter, and HMS *Brilliant* launched a Westland Lynx HAS Mk 2. The Lynx launched a torpedo, and strafed the submarine with its pintle-mounted general purpose machine gun; the Wessex also fired on the *Santa Fe* with its GPMG. The Wasp from *Plymouth* as well as two other Wasps launched from HMS *Endurance* fired AS-12 ASM antiship missiles at the submarine, scoring hits. *Santa Fe* was damaged badly enough to prevent her from submerging. The crew abandoned the submarine at the jetty at King Edward Point on South Georgia.

With the *Tidespring* now far out to sea and the Argentine forces augmented by the submarine's crew, Major Sheridan decided to gather the 76 men he had and make a direct assault that day.

After a short forced march by the British troops, the Argentine forces surrendered without resistance. The message sent from the naval force at South Georgia to London was, "Be pleased to inform Her Majesty that the White Ensign flies alongside the Union Jack in South Georgia. God Save the Queen." The Prime Minister, Margaret Thatcher, broke the news to the media, telling them to "Just rejoice at that news!"

Black Buck raids

RAF Avro Vulcan B.Mk.2 strategic bomber.

On 1 May British operations on the Falklands opened with the "Black Buck 1" attack (of a series of five) on the airfield at Stanley. A Vulcan bomber from Ascension flew on an 8,000-nautical-mile (15,000 km; 9,200 mi) round trip dropping conventional bombs across the runway at Stanley and back to Ascension. The mission required repeated refuelling, and required several Victor tanker aircraft operating in concert, including tanker to tanker refuelling. The overall effect of the raids on the war is difficult to determine, and the raids consumed precious tanker resources from Ascension. The raids did minimal damage to the runway and damage to radars was quickly repaired. Commonly dismissed as post-war propaganda, Argentine sources were originally the source of claims that the Vulcan raids influenced Argentina to withdraw some of its Mirage IIIs from Southern Argentina to the Buenos Aires Defence Zone. This dissuasive effect was however watered down when British officials made clear that there would be no strikes on air bases in Argentina.

Of the five Black Buck raids, three were against Stanley Airfield, with the other two anti-radar missions using Shrike anti-radiation missiles.

Escalation of the air war

Royal Navy Fleet Air Arm Sea Harrier FRS1. The flamboyant paint scheme was altered to a duller one en route South.

The Falklands had only three airfields. The longest and only paved runway was at the capital, Stanley, and even that was too short to support fast jets. Therefore, the Argentines were forced to launch their major strikes from the mainland, severely hampering their efforts at forward staging, combat air patrols and close air support over the islands. The effective loiter time of incoming Argentine aircraft was low, and they were later compelled to overfly British forces in any attempt to attack the islands.

The first major Argentine strike force comprised 36 aircraft (McDonnell Douglas A-4 Skyhawks, Israel Aircraft Industries Daggers, English Electric B Mk 62 Canberras, and Dassault Mirage III escorts), and was sent on 1 May, in the belief that the British invasion was imminent or landings had already taken place. Only a section of Grupo 6 (flying IAI Dagger aircraft) found ships, which were firing at Argentine defences near the islands. The Daggers managed to attack the ships and return safely. This greatly boosted morale of the Argentine pilots, who now knew they could survive an attack against modern warships, protected by radar ground clutter from the Islands and by using a late *pop-up* profile.

Meanwhile, other Argentine aircraft were intercepted by BAE Sea Harriers operating from HMS *Invincible*. A Dagger (piloted by Osvaldo Ardiles' cousin José) and a Canberra were shot down.

Argentine Air Force Mirage IIIEA. Their lack of aerial refuelling capability prevented them from being used effectively over the islands in the air-air role.

A Royal Navy Sea King helicopter rescues Sqn Ldr Jerry Pook, after he was forced to bail out over the sea. His Harrier GR.3 had been hit by ground fire west of Stanley on 30 May.

Sinking of ARA *General Belgrano*

The ARA *General Belgrano*, sinking.

Combat broke out between Sea Harrier FRS Mk 1 fighters of No. 801 Naval Air Squadron and Mirage III fighters of Grupo 8. Both sides refused to fight at the other's best altitude, until two Mirages finally descended to engage. One was shot down by an AIM-9L Sidewinder air-to-air missile (AAM), while the other escaped but was damaged and without enough fuel to return to its mainland air base. The plane made for Stanley, where it fell victim to friendly fire from the Argentine defenders.

As a result of this experience, Argentine Air Force staff decided to employ A-4 Skyhawks and Daggers only as strike units, the Canberras only during the night, and Mirage IIIs (without air refuelling capability or any capable AAM) as decoys to lure away the British Sea Harriers. The decoying would be later extended with the formation of the Escuadron Fenix, a squadron of civilian jets flying 24 hours-a-day simulating strike aircraft preparing to attack the fleet. On one of these flights, an Air Force Learjet was shot down, killing the squadron commander, Vice Commodore Rodolfo De La Colina, the highest-ranking Argentine officer to die in the war.

Stanley was used as an Argentine strongpoint throughout the conflict. Despite the Black Buck and Harrier raids on Stanley airfield (no fast jets were stationed there for air defence) and overnight shelling by detached ships, it was never out of action entirely. Stanley was defended by a mixture of surface-to-air missile (SAM) systems (Franco-German Roland and British Tigercat) and Swiss-built Oerlikon 35 mm twin anti-aircraft cannons. Lockheed Hercules transport night flights brought supplies, weapons, vehicles, and fuel, and airlifted out the wounded up until the end of the conflict. The few RN Sea Harriers were considered too valuable by day to risk in night-time blockade operations, and their Blue Fox radar was not an effective look-down over land radar.

The only Argentine Hercules shot down by the British was lost on 1 June when TC-63 was intercepted by a Sea Harrier in daylight when it was searching for the British fleet north-east of the islands after the Argentine Navy retired its last SP-2H Neptune due to airframe attrition.

Various options to attack the home base of the five Argentine Etendards at Río Grande were examined and discounted (Operation Mikado), subsequently five Royal Navy submarines lined up, submerged, on the edge of Argentina's 12-nautical-mile (22 km; 14 mi) territorial limit to provide early warning of bombing raids on the British task force.

Two separate British naval task forces (surface vessels and submarines) and the Argentine fleet were operating in the neighbourhood of the Falklands, and soon came into conflict. The first naval loss was the World War II vintage Argentine light cruiser ARA *General Belgrano*. The nuclear-powered submarine HMS *Conqueror* sank the *Belgrano* on 2 May. Three hundred and twenty-three members of *Belgrano*'s crew died in the incident. Over 700 men were rescued from the open ocean despite cold seas and stormy weather. The losses from *Belgrano* totalled just over half of the Argentine deaths in the Falklands conflict and the loss of the ARA *General Belgrano* hardened the stance of the Argentine government.

Regardless of controversies over the sinking, it had a crucial strategic effect: the elimination of the Argentine naval threat. After her loss, the entire Argentine fleet, with the exception of the conventional submarine ARA *San Luis*, returned to port and did not leave again for the duration of hostilities. The two escorting destroyers and the battle group centred on the aircraft carrier ARA *Veinticinco de Mayo* both withdrew from the area, ending the direct threat to the British fleet that their pincer movement had represented.

In a separate incident later that night, British forces engaged an Argentine patrol gunboat, the ARA *Alferez Sobral*. At the time, the *Alferez Sobral* was searching for the crew of the Argentine Air Force English Electric Canberra light bomber shot down on 1 May. Two Royal Navy Lynx helicopters fired four Sea Skua missiles against her. Badly damaged and with eight crew dead, the

Sobral managed to return to Puerto Deseado two days later, but the Canberra's crew were never found.

Sinking of HMS *Sheffield*

French-built Super Etendard of the Argentine Naval Aviation.

On 4 May, two days after the sinking of *Belgrano*, the British lost the Type 42 destroyer HMS *Sheffield* to fire following an Exocet missile strike from the Argentine 2nd Naval Air Fighter/Attack Squadron. *Sheffield* had been ordered forward with two other Type 42s to provide a long-range radar and medium-high altitude missile picket far from the British carriers. She was struck amidships, with devastating effect, ultimately killing 20 crew members and severely injuring 24 others. The ship was abandoned several hours later, gutted and deformed by the fires that continued to burn for six more days. She finally sank outside the Maritime Exclusion Zone on 10 May.

The incident is described in detail by Admiral Sandy Woodward in his book *One Hundred Days*, Chapter One. Woodward was a former commanding officer of *Sheffield*.

The tempo of operations increased throughout the second half of May as United Nations attempts to mediate a peace were rejected by the British, who felt that any delay would make a campaign impractical in the South Atlantic storms. The destruction of *Sheffield* had a profound impact on the British public, bringing home the fact that the "Falklands Crisis", as the BBC News put it, was now an actual "shooting war".

SAS operations

Given the threat to the British fleet posed by the Etendard-Exocet combination, plans were made to use Special Air Service troops to attack the home base of the five Etendards at Río Grande, Tierra del Fuego. The operation was code named "Mikado". The aim was to destroy the missiles and the aircraft that carried them, and to kill the pilots in their quarters. Two plans were drafted and underwent preliminary rehearsal: a landing by approximately fifty-five SAS in two C-130 Hercules aircraft directly on the runway at Rio Grande; and infiltration of twenty-four SAS by inflatable boats brought within a few miles of the coast by submarine. Neither plan was implemented; the earlier airborne assault plan attracted considerable hostility from some members of the SAS, who considered the proposed raid a suicide mission. Ironically, the Rio Grande area would be defended by four full-strength battalions of Marine Infantry of the Argentine Marine Corps of the Argentine Navy some of whose officers were trained in the UK by the SBS years earlier.

After the war, Argentine marine commanders admitted that they were waiting for some kind of landing by SAS forces but never expected a Hercules to land directly on their runways. However they would have tried to pursue British forces even into Chilean territory if they were attacked.

An SAS reconnaissance team was dispatched to carry out preparations for a seaborne infiltration. A Westland Sea King helicopter carrying the assigned team took off from HMS *Invincible* on the night of 17 May, but bad weather forced it to land 50 miles (80 km) from its target, and the mission was aborted. The pilot flew to Chile and dropped off the SAS team, before setting fire to his helicopter and surrendering to the Chilean authorities. The discovery of the burnt-out helicopter attracted considerable international attention at the time.

On 14 May the SAS carried out the raid on Pebble Island at the Falklands, where the Argentine Navy had taken over a grass airstrip for FMA IA 58 Pucará light ground attack aircraft and T-34 Mentors. The raid destroyed the aircraft there.

Landing at San Carlos—Bomb Alley

An Argentine Air Force A-4C Skyhawk flying to the islands. Note the 494 kg bomb

During the night on 21 May the British Amphibious Task Group under the command of Commodore Michael Clapp (Commodore, Amphibious Warfare – COMAW) mounted *Operation Sutton*, the amphibious landing on beaches around San Carlos Water, on the northwestern coast of East Falkland facing onto Falkland Sound. The bay, known as *Bomb Alley* by British forces, was the scene of repeated air attacks by low-flying Argentine jets.

The 4,000 men of 3 Commando Brigade were put ashore as follows: 2nd battalion of the Parachute Regiment (2 Para) from the RORO ferry *Norland* and 40 Commando (Royal Marines) from the amphibious ship HMS *Fearless* were landed at San Carlos (Blue Beach), 3 Para from the amphibious ship HMS *Intrepid* were landed at Port San Carlos (Green Beach) and 45 Commando from RFA *Stromness* were landed at Ajax Bay (Red Beach). Notably the waves of 8 LCUs and 8 LCVPs were led by Major Ewen Southby-Tailyour who had commanded the Falklands detachment only a year previously. 42 Commando on the ocean liner SS *Canberra* was a tactical reserve. Units from the Royal Artillery, Royal Engineers etc. and tanks were also put ashore with the landing craft, the Round table class LSL and mexeflote barges. Rapier missile launchers were carried as underslung loads of Sea Kings for rapid deployment.

By dawn the next day they had established a secure beachhead from which to conduct offensive operations. From there Brigadier Thompson's plan was to capture Darwin and Goose Green before turning towards Port Stanley. Now, with the British troops on the ground, the Argentine Air Force began the night bombing campaign against them using Canberra bomber planes until the last day of the war (14 June).

HMS *Antelope* smoking after being hit, 23 May

At sea, the paucity of the British ships' anti-aircraft defences was demonstrated in the sinking of HMS *Ardent* on 21 May, HMS *Antelope* on 24 May, and MV *Atlantic Conveyor* (struck by two AM39 Exocets) on 25 May along with a vital cargo of helicopters, runway-building equipment and tents. The loss of all but one of the Chinook helicopters being carried by the Atlantic Conveyor was a severe blow from a logistics perspective. Also lost on this day was HMS *Coventry*, a sister to HMS *Sheffield*, whilst in company with HMS *Broadsword* after being ordered to act as decoy to draw away Argentine aircraft from other ships at San Carlos Bay. HMS *Argonaut* and HMS *Brilliant* were badly damaged. However, many British ships escaped terminal damage because of the Argentine pilots' bombing tactics.

To avoid the highest concentration of British air defences, Argentine pilots released ordnance from very low altitude, and hence their bomb fuzes did not have sufficient time to arm before impact. The low release of the retarded bombs (some of which had been sold to the Argentines by the British years earlier) meant that many never exploded, as there was insufficient time in the air for them to arm themselves. A simple free-fall bomb will, during a low altitude release, impact almost directly below the aircraft which is then within the lethal fragmentation zone of the resulting explosion. A retarded bomb has a small parachute or air brake that opens to reduce the speed of the bomb to produce a safe horizontal separation between the two. The fuze for a retarded bomb requires a minimum time over which the retarder is open to ensure safe separation. The pilots would have been aware of this, but due to the high concentration levels required to avoid SAMs and AAA, as well as any British Sea Harriers, many failed to climb to the necessary release point. The problem was solved by the improvised fitting of retarding devices, allowing low-level bombing attacks as employed on 8 June.

In his autobiographical account of the Falklands War, Admiral Woodward blames the BBC World Service for these changes to the bombs. The World Service reported the lack of detonations after receiving a briefing on the matter from a Ministry of Defence official. He describes the BBC as being more concerned with being "fearless seekers after truth" than with the lives of British servicemen. Colonel 'H'. Jones levelled similar accusations against the BBC after they disclosed the impending British attack on Goose Green by 2 Para. Jones had threatened to lead the prosecution of senior BBC officials for treason but was unable to do so since he was himself killed in action around Goose Green.

Thirteen bombs hit British ships without detonating. Lord Craig, the retired Marshal of the Royal Air Force, is said to have remarked: "Six better fuses and we would have lost" although *Ardent* and *Antelope* were both lost despite the failure of bombs to explode. The fuzes were functioning correctly, and the bombs were simply released from too low an altitude. The Argentines lost 22 aircraft in the attacks.

Battle of Goose Green

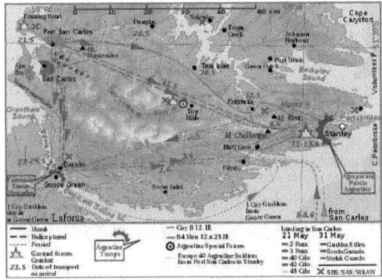

Infantry deployment in East Falklands after Landing in San Carlos

From early on 27 May until 28 May, 2 Para, (approximately 500 men) with artillery support from 8 (Alma) Commando Battery (Royal Artillery), approached and attacked Darwin and Goose Green, which was held by the Argentine 12th Infantry Regiment. After a tough struggle that lasted all night and into the next day, 17 British and 47 Argentine soldiers were killed. In total 961 Argentine troops (including 202 Argentine Air Force personnel of the *Condor* airfield) were taken prisoners.

The BBC announced the taking of Goose Green on the BBC World Service before it had actually happened. It was during this attack that Lieutenant Colonel H. Jones, the commanding officer of 2 Para was killed while charging into the well-prepared Argentine positions at the head of his battalion. He was posthumously awarded the Victoria Cross.

With the sizeable Argentine force at Goose Green out of the way, British forces were now able to break out of the San Carlos bridgehead. On 27 May, men of 45 Cdo and 3 Para started a loaded march across East Falkland towards the coastal settlement of Teal Inlet.

Special forces on Mount Kent

Meanwhile, 42 Commando prepared to move by helicopter to Mount Kent. Unknown to senior British officers, the Argentine generals were determined to tie down the British troops in the Mount Kent area, and on 27 May and 28 May they sent transport aircraft loaded with

Blowpipe surface-to-air missiles and commandos (602nd Commando Company and 601st National Gendarmerie Special Forces Squadron) to Stanley. This operation was known as Operation AUTOIMPUESTA (Self-Determination-Initiative).

For the next week, the Special Air Service (SAS) and Mountain and Arctic Warfare Cadre of 3 Commando Brigade waged intense patrol battles with patrols of the volunteers' 602nd Commando Company under Major Aldo Rico, normally 2IC of the 22nd Mountain Infantry Regiment. Throughout 30 May, Royal Air Force Harriers were active over Mount Kent. One of them, Harrier *XZ963*, flown by Squadron Leader Jerry Pook—in responding to a call for help from D Squadron, attacked Mount Kent's eastern lower slopes, and that led to its loss through small-arms fire. Pook was subsequently awarded the Distinguished Flying Cross.

The Argentine Navy used their last AM39 Exocet missile attempting to attack HMS *Invincible* on 30 May. There are claims the missile struck, however the British have denied this, some citing that HMS *Avenger* shot it down.

On 31 May, the Royal Marines Mountain and Arctic Warfare Cadre (M&AWC) defeated Argentine Special Forces at the Battle of Top Malo House. A 13-strong Argentine Army Commando detachment (Captain José Vercesi's 1st Assault Section, 602nd Commando Company) found itself trapped in a small shepherd's house at Top Malo. The Argentine commandos fired from windows and doorways and then took refuge in a stream bed 200 metres (700 ft) from the burning house. Completely surrounded, they fought 19 M&AWC marines under Captain Rod Boswell for forty-five minutes until, with their ammunition almost exhausted, they elected to surrender.

Three Cadre members were badly wounded. On the Argentine side there were two dead including Lieutenant Ernesto Espinoza and Sergeant Mateo Sbert (who were decorated for their bravery). Only five Argentines were left unscathed. As the British mopped up Top Malo House, down from Malo Hill came Lieutenant Fraser Haddow's M&AWC patrol, brandishing a large Union Flag. One wounded Argentine soldier, Lieutenant Horacio Losito, commented that their escape route would have taken them through Haddow's position.

Major Mario Castagneto's 601st Commandos tried to move forward on Kawasaki motorbikes and commandeered Land Rovers to rescue 602nd Commando Company on Estancia Mountain. Spotted by 42 Commando of the Royal Marines, they were engaged with 81mm mortars and forced to withdraw to Two Sisters mountain. Captain Eduardo Villarruel on Estancia Mountain realised his position had become untenable and after conferring with fellow officers ordered a withdrawal.

The Argentine operation also saw the extensive use of helicopter support to position and extract patrols; the 601st Combat Aviation Battalion also suffered casualties. At about 11.00 am on 30 May, an Aerospatiale SA-330 Puma helicopter was brought down by a shoulder-launched Stinger surface-to-air missile (SAM) fired by the SAS in the vicinity of Mount Kent. Six National Gendarmerie Special Forces were killed and eight more wounded in the crash.

As Brigadier Julian Thompson commented, "It was fortunate that I had ignored the views expressed by Northwood that reconnaissance of Mount Kent before insertion of 42 Commando was superfluous. Had D Squadron not been there, the Argentine Special Forces would have caught the Commando before deplaning and, in the darkness and confusion on a strange landing zone, inflicted heavy casualties on men and helicopters."

Bluff Cove and Fitzroy

The abandoned hulk of RFA *Sir Tristram* in Fitzroy.

By 1 June, with the arrival of a further 5,000 British troops of the 5th Infantry Brigade, the new British divisional commander, Major General Jeremy Moore RM, had sufficient force to start planning an offensive against Stanley.

During this build-up, the Argentine air assaults on the British naval forces continued, killing 56. Of the dead, 32 were from the Welsh Guards on RFA *Sir Galahad* and RFA *Sir Tristram* on 8 June. According to Surgeon-Commander Rick Jolly of the Falklands Field Hospital, more than 150 men suffered burns and injuries of some kind in the attack, including, famously, Simon Weston.

The Guards were sent to support a *dashing* advance along the southern approach to Stanley. On 2 June a small advance party of 2 Para moved to Swan Inlet house in a number of Army Westland Scout helicopters. Telephoning ahead to Fitzroy, they discovered the area clear of Argentines and (exceeding their authority) commandeered the one remaining RAF Chinook helicopter to frantically ferry another contingent of 2 Para ahead to Fitzroy (a settlement on Port Pleasant) and Bluff Cove (a settlement confusingly, and perhaps ultimately fatally, on Port Fitzroy).

This uncoordinated advance caused planning nightmares for the commanders of the combined operation, as they now found themselves with a 30 miles (48 km) string of indefensible positions on their southern flank. Support could not be sent by air as the single remaining Chinook was already heavily oversubscribed. The soldiers could march, but their equipment and heavy supplies would need to be ferried by sea. Plans were drawn up for half the Welsh Guards to march light on the night of 2 June, whilst the Scots Guards and the second half of the Welsh Guards were to be ferried from San Carlos Water in the Landing Ship Logistics (LSL) *Sir Tristram* and the landing platform dock (LPD) *Intrepid* on the night of 5 June. *Intrepid* was planned to stay one day and unload itself and as much of *Sir Tristram* as possible, leaving the next evening for the relative safety of San Carlos. Escorts would be provided for this day, after which *Sir Tristram* would be left to unload using a Mexeflote (a powered raft) for as long as it took to finish.

Political pressure from above to not risk the LPD forced Commodore Clapp to alter this plan. Two lower-value LSLs would be sent, but without suitable beaches on which to land, *Intrepid*'s landing craft would need to accompany them to unload. A complicated operation across several nights with *Intrepid* and her sister ship *Fearless* sailing half-way to dispatch their craft was devised. The attempted overland march by half the Welsh Guards failed, possibly as they refused to march light and attempted to carry their equipment. They returned to San Carlos and were landed directly at Bluff Cove when *Fearless* dispatched her landing craft. *Sir Tristram* sailed on the night of 6 June and was joined by *Sir Galahad* at dawn on 7 June. Anchored 1,200 feet (370 m) apart in Port Pleasant, the landing ships were near Fitzroy, the designated landing point.

The landing craft should have been able to unload the ships to that point relatively quickly, but confusion over the ordered disembarcation point (the first half of the Guards going direct to Bluff Cove) resulted in the senior Welsh Guards infantry officer aboard insisting his troops be ferried the far longer distance directly to Port Fitzroy/Bluff Cove. The alternative was for the infantrymen to march via the recently repaired Bluff Cove bridge (destroyed by retreating Argentine combat engineers) to their destination, a journey of around seven miles (11 km).

On *Sir Galahad*'s stern ramp there was an argument about what to do. The officers on board were told they could not sail to Bluff Cove that day. They were told they had to get their men off ship and onto the beach as soon as possible as the ships were vulnerable to enemy aircraft. It would take 20 minutes to transport the men to shore using the LCU and Mexeflote. They would then have the choice to walk the 7 miles to Bluff Cove or wait until dark to sail there. The officers on board said they would remain on board until dark and then sail. They refused to take their men off the ship. They possibly doubted that the bridge had been repaired due to the presence on board *Sir Galahad* of the Royal Engineer Troop whose job it was to repair the bridge. The Welsh Guards were keen to rejoin the rest of their Battalion who were potentially facing the enemy without their support. They had also not seen any enemy aircraft since landing at San Carlos and may have been over confident in the air defences. Ewen Southby-Tailyour gave a direct order for the men to leave the ship and go to the beach. The order was ignored.

The longer journey time of the landing craft taking the troops directly to Bluff Cove and the squabbling over how the landing was to be performed caused enormous delay in unloading. This had disastrous consequences. Without escorts, having not yet established their air defence, and still almost fully laden, the two LSLs in Port Pleasant were sitting targets for two waves of Argentine A-4 Skyhawks.

The disaster at Port Pleasant (although often known as Bluff Cove) would provide the world with some of the most sobering images of the war as TV news video footage showed Navy helicopters hovering in thick smoke to winch survivors from the burning landing ships. British casualties were 48 killed and 115 wounded. Three Argentine pilots were also killed. However, Argentine General Mario Menendez, commander of Argentine forces in the Falklands, was told that 900 British soldiers had died. He expected that the losses would cause enemy morale to drop and the British assault to stall.

Fall of Stanley

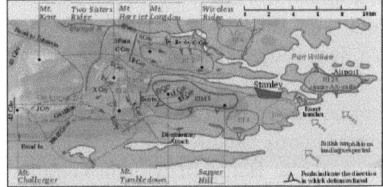

The road to Stanley

Notable battles:
- Battle of Mount Harriet
- Battle of Mount Longdon
- Battle of Wireless Ridge
- Battle of Mount Tumbledown
- Battle of Two Sisters

On the night of 11 June, after several days of painstaking reconnaissance and logistic build-up, British forces launched a brigade-sized night attack against the heavily defended ring of high ground surrounding Stanley. After 3 Para took Port Stanley, units of 3 Commando Brigade, supported by naval gunfire from several Royal Navy ships, simultaneously assaulted in the Battle of Mount Harriet, Battle of Two Sisters, and Battle of Mount Longdon. Mount Harriet was taken at a cost of 2 British and 18 Argentine soldiers. At Two Sisters, the British faced both enemy resistance and friendly fire, but managed to capture their objectives. The toughest battle was at Mount Longdon. British forces were bogged down by assault rifle, mortar, machine gun, artillery fire, sniper fire, and ambushes. Despite this, the British continued their advance.

During this battle, 13 were killed when HMS *Glamorgan*, straying too close to shore while returning from the gun line, was struck by an improvised trailer-based Exocet MM38 launcher taken from ARA *Seguí* destroyer by Argentine Navy technicians. On this day, Sgt Ian McKay of 4 Platoon, B Company, 3 Para died in a grenade attack on an Argentine bunker, which earned him a posthumous Victoria Cross. After a night of fierce fighting, all objectives were secured. Both sides suffered heavy losses.

The night of 13 June saw the start of the second phase of attacks, in which the momentum of the initial assault was maintained. 2 Para with CVRT support from The Blues and Royals, captured Wireless Ridge at the Battle of Wireless Ridge, at a loss of 3 British and 25 Argentine dead, and the 2nd battalion, Scots Guards captured Mount Tumbledown at the Battle of Mount Tumbledown, which cost 10 British and 30 Argentines dead.

A pile of discarded Argentine weapons in Port Stanley.

With the last natural defence line at Mount Tumbledown breached, the Argentine town defences of Stanley began to falter. In the morning gloom, one company commander got lost and his junior officers became despondent. Private Santiago Carrizo of the 3rd Regiment described how a platoon commander ordered them to take up positions in the houses and "if a Kelper resists, shoot him", but the entire company did nothing of the kind.

A cease fire was declared on 14 June and the commander of the Argentine garrison in Stanley, Brigade General Mario Menéndez surrendered to Major General Jeremy Moore the same day.

Surrender of Corbeta Uruguay

On 20 June the British retook the South Sandwich Islands, (which involved accepting the surrender of the Southern Thule Garrison at the *Corbeta Uruguay* base) and declared hostilities to be over. Argentina had established Corbeta Uruguay in 1976, but prior to 1982 the United Kingdom had contested the existence of the Argentine base only through diplomatic channels.

Casualties

The Argentine Military Cemetery, on East Falkland.

The British Military Cemetery at San Carlos on East Falkland.

'Monumento a los Caídos en Malvinas' (Monument for the fallen in the Falklands) in Plaza San Martín, Buenos Aires; a member of the historic *Patricios* regiment stands guard.

In total 907 were killed during the 74 days of the conflict:
- **Argentina** – 649
  - Ejército Argentino (*Army*) – 194 (16 officers, 35 NCOs and 143 conscript privates)
  - Armada de la República Argentina (*Navy*) – 341 (including 321 in *Belgrano* and 4 naval aviators)
    - IMARA (*Marines*) – 34
  - Fuerza Aérea Argentina (*Air Force*) – 55 (including 31 pilots and 14 ground crew)
  - Gendarmería Nacional Argentina (*Border Guard*) – 7
  - Prefectura Naval Argentina (*Coast Guard*) – 2
  - Civilian sailors – 16
- **United Kingdom** – A total of 255 British servicemen and 3 female Falklands Island civilians were killed during the Falklands War.
  - Royal Navy – 86 + 2 Hong Kong laundrymen (see below)
  - Royal Marines – 27 (2 officers, 14 NCOs and 11 marines)
  - Royal Fleet Auxiliary – 4 + 4 Hong Kong laundrymen
  - Merchant Navy – 6 + 2 Hong Kong sailors
  - British Army – 123 (7 officers, 40 NCOs and 76 privates)
  - Royal Air Force – 1 (1 officer)
  - Falklands Islands civilians – 3 women killed by friendly fire

Of the 86 Royal Navy personnel, 22 were lost in HMS *Ardent*, 19 + 1 lost in HMS *Sheffield*, 19 + 1 lost in HMS *Coventry* and 13 lost in HMS *Glamorgan*. Fourteen naval cooks were among the dead, the largest number from any one branch in the Royal Navy.

Thirty-three of the British Army's dead came from the Welsh Guards, 21 from the 3rd Battalion, the Parachute Regiment, 18 from the 2nd Battalion, the Parachute Regiment, 19 from the Special Air Service (SAS), 3 from Royal Signals and 8 from each of the Scots Guards and Royal Engineers Only one dead was from the 1st battalion/7th Duke of Edinburgh's Own Gurkha Rifles.

Two more British deaths may be attributed to Operation Corporate, bringing the total to 260:
- Captain Brian Biddick from HMHS *Uganda* underwent an emergency operation on the voyage to the Falklands, was repatriated by an RAF medical flight to the hospital at Wroughton where he died on 12 May.
- Paul Mills from HMS *Coventry* suffered from complications from a skull fracture sustained in the

sinking of his ship and died on 29 March 1983; he is buried in his home town of Swavesey.

Memorials

As well as memorials on the islands, there is a memorial to the British war dead in the crypt of St Paul's Cathedral, London. There is a memorial at Plaza San Martín in Buenos Aires for the Argentine war dead, another one in Rosario, and a third one in Ushuaia.

During the war, British dead were put into plastic body bags and buried in mass graves. After the war, the bodies were removed with 14 reburied at Blue Beach Military Cemetery and 64 returned to Britain. Argentine dead were reburied at the Argentine Military Cemetery west of the Darwin Settlement. The United Kingdom offered to send the bodies back to Argentina, but Argentina refused, knowing that the remains would ensure a continuing Argentine presence on the islands.

There were 1,188 Argentine and 777 British non-fatal casualties. Further information about the field hospitals and hospital ships is at Ajax Bay, List of hospitals and hospital ships of the Royal Navy, HMS *Hydra*. On the Argentine side beside the Military Hospital at Port Stanley, the Argentine Air Force Mobile Field Hospital was deployed at Comodoro Rivadavia and the Argentine Navy ships ARA *Almirante Irizar* and ARA *Bahia Paraiso* were converted to Hospital ships

Although some have been cleared, a substantial number of minefields still exist in the islands, such as this one at Port William on East Falkland.

There are still 117 uncleared minefields on the Falkland Islands and UXOs are scattered all over the battlefields due to the soft peat ground. No human casualties from mines or UXO have been reported in the Falkland Islands since 1984, and no civilian mine casualties have ever occurred on the islands. The UK reported six military personnel were injured in 1982 and a further two injured in 1983. Most military accidents took place while clearing the minefields in the immediate aftermath of the 1982 conflict or in the process of trying to establish the extent of the minefield perimeters, particularly where no detailed records existed.
See also Argentine and British ground forces in the Falklands War

Aftermath

This brief war brought many consequences for all the parties involved, besides the great loss of human life and materiel.

In the United Kingdom, Margaret Thatcher won the time and support she required for her economic measures (which tackled inflation but sent unemployment to its highest postwar levels) to take effect, national pride received a big boost of confidence and assurance, the Royal Navy proved its value once more. The success of the Falklands campaign was widely regarded as the factor in the turnaround in fortunes for the Conservative government, who had been trailing behind the SDP-Liberal Alliance in the opinion polls for months before the conflict began, but after the success in the Falklands the Conservatives returned to the top of the opinion polls by a wide margin and went on to win the following year's general election by a landslide.

Subsequently, Defence Secretary Nott's proposed cuts to the Royal Navy were abandoned.

The islanders subsequently had full British citizenship restored in 1983, their lifestyle was improved by investments Britain made after the war and the liberalisation of economic measures that had been stalled through fear of angering Argentina. In 1985, a new constitution was enacted promoting self-government, which has continued to devolve power to the islanders.

The war for Argentina also had an effect in the form of avoiding a possible war with Chile and, more importantly, the return of democracy with the 1983 first free general elections since 1973. It had a major social impact, destroying the military's image as the *moral reserve of the nation* that they had maintained through most of the 20th century.

Public relations

Argentina

Gente's "Estamos ganando" headline ("We're winning").

Selected war correspondents were regularly flown to Port Stanley in military aircraft to report on the war. Back in Buenos Aires newspapers and magazines faithfully reported on "the heroic actions of the largely conscript army and its successes".

Officers from the intelligence services were attached to the newspapers and 'leaked' information confirming the official communiqués from the government. The glossy magazines *Gente* and *Siete Días* swelled to sixty pages with colour photographs of British warships in flames – many of them faked – and bogus eyewitness reports of the Argentine commandos' guerrilla war on South Georgia (6 May) and an already dead Pucará pilot's attack on HMS *Hermes* (Lt. Daniel Antonio Jukic had been killed at Goose Green during a British air strike on 1 May). Most of the faked photos actually came from the tabloid press. One of the best remembered headlines was "Estamos ganando" ("We're winning") from the magazine Gente, that would later use variations of it.

The Argentine troops on the Falkland Islands could read *Gaceta Argentina*—a newspaper intended to boost morale among the servicemen. Some of its untruths could easily be unveiled by the soldiers who recovered corpses.

The *Malvinas course* united the Argentines in a patriotic atmosphere that protected the junta from critics, and even opponents of the military government supported Galtieri; Ernesto Sabato said: "*Don't be mistaken, Europe; it is not a dictatorship who is fighting for the Malvinas, it is the whole Nation. Opponents of the military dictatorship, like me, are fighting to extirpate the last trace of colonialism.*" The *Madres de Plaza de Mayo* were even exposed to death threats from ordinary people.

HMS *Invincible* was repeatedly sunk in the Argentine press, and on 30 April 1982 the Argentine magazine *Tal Cual* showed UK's PM Thatcher with an eyepatch and the text: *Pirate, witch and assassin. Guilty!*

Three British reporters sent to Argentina to cover the war from the 'other side' were jailed until the end of the war.

United Kingdom

The Sun's "Gotcha" headline.

Seventeen newspaper reporters, two photographers, two radio reporters and three television reporters with five technicians sailed with the Task Force to the war. The Newspaper Publishers' Association selected them from among 160 applicants, excluding foreign media. Due to the hasty departure, not all of them were "the right stuff"; two journalists on HMS *Invincible* were interested in nothing but Queen Elizabeth II's son Prince Andrew.

Merchant vessels had the civilian Inmarsat uplink, which enabled written telex and voice report transmissions via satellite. Canberra had a facsimile machine that was used to upload 202 pictures from the South Atlantic over the course of the war. The Royal Navy leased bandwidth on the US Defense Satellite Communications System for worldwide communications. Television demands a thousand times the data rate of telephone, but the Ministry of Defence was unsuccessful in convincing the US to allocate more bandwidth. TV producers suspected that the enquiry was half-hearted; since the Vietnam War television pictures of casualties and traumatised soldiers were recognised as having negative propaganda value. However the technology only allowed uploading a single frame per 20 minutes – and only if the military satellites were allocated 100% to television transmissions. Videotapes were shipped to Ascension Island, where a broadband satellite uplink was available, resulting in TV coverage being delayed by three weeks.

The press was very dependent on the Royal Navy, and was censored on site. Many reporters in the UK knew more about the war than those with the Task Force.

The Royal Navy expected Fleet Street to conduct a World War Two style positive news campaign but the majority of the British media, especially the BBC, reported the war in a neutral fashion. These reporters referred to "the British troops" and "the Argentinian troops" instead of "our lads" and the dehumanised "Argies". The two main tabloid papers presented opposing viewpoints: *The Daily Mirror* was decidedly anti-war, whilst *The Sun* became notorious for its jingoistic and xenophobic headlines, including 20 April headline "Stick It Up Your Junta!", and was condemned for the "Gotcha" headline following the sinking of the ARA *General Belgrano*.

Cultural impact

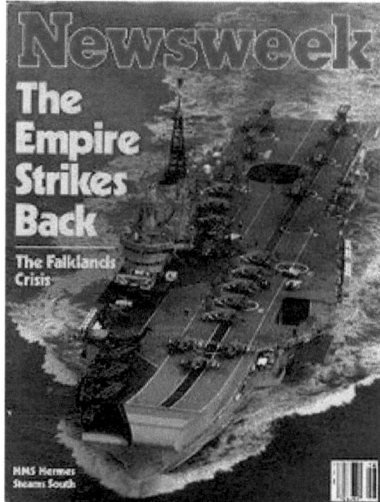

Newsweek magazine cover, 19 April 1982. HMS *Hermes* pictured.

There were wide-ranging influences on popular culture in both the UK and Argentina, from the immediate postwar period to the present. The words *yomp* and *Exocet* entered the British vernacular as a result of the war. The Falklands War also provided material for theatre, film and TV drama and influenced the output of musicians.

Source (edited): "http://en.wikipedia.org/wiki/Falklands_War"

Finchley (UK Parliament constituency)

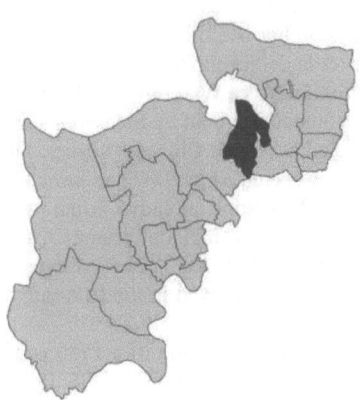

Finchley constituency within the parliamentary county of Middlesex, showing boundaries used from 1918-45.

Finchley constituency within the parliamentary county of Middlesex, showing boundaries used from 1945-50.

Finchley was a constituency represented in the House of Commons of the Parliament of the United Kingdom. It elected one Member of Parliament (MP) by the first past the post system of election; its best-known MP was Margaret Thatcher, Prime Minister from 1979 to 1990. It was abolished in 1997.

Boundaries

In 1918 the constituency was created as a county division of Middlesex, centred on the town of Finchley, which before 1918 had been located in the Hornsey constituency. The local government areas included in the seat were the Finchley and Friern Barnet Urban Districts. In 1934 the Finchley district became a Municipal Borough.

In 1945 there was an interim redistribution of parliamentary constituencies to split those with more than 100,000 electors, prior to the general redistribution of 1950. Middlesex was significantly affected by the interim changes. This constituency had a minor revision. In the 1945-1950 Parliament it included the Municipal Borough of Finchley, part of the Municipal Borough of Hornsey, and part of the Friern Barnet Urban District.

In the redistribution of 1950, the seat was re-classified as a borough constituency. The boundaries reverted to those of 1945, with the constituency comprising the Municipal Borough of Finchley and the Friern Barnet Urban District.

In 1965 the area of the constituency was joined to other districts to form the London Borough of Barnet in Greater London.

In the 1974 changes to parliamentary boundaries, the constituency was redefined as comprising the wards of East Finchley, Finchley, Friern Barnet, St Paul's, and Woodhouse. The boundaries were left unchanged in the 1983 redistribution.

Source (edited): "http://en.wikipedia.org/wiki/Finchley_(UK_Parliament_constituency)"

Iron Lady

Iron Lady is a nickname that has frequently been used to describe female heads of government around the world. The term describes a "strong willed" woman. This iron metaphor was most famously applied to Margaret Thatcher, nicknamed so in 1976 by the Soviet media for her staunch opposition to communism.

Use in politics

Leaders who have earned the unofficial title (some of them postfactum) include:
- Margaret Thatcher, the Prime Minister of the United Kingdom from 1979 to 1990
- Barbara Castle, a prominent British Labour Party politician, whose active political career spanned over 40 years.
- Indira Gandhi, the Prime Minister of India from 1966 to 1977 and from 1980 to 1984
- Golda Meir, the Prime Minister of Israel from 1969 to 1974
- Gloria Macapagal-Arroyo, the second woman President of the Philippines from 2001 to 2010, dubbed as the "Iron Lady of Asia"
- Wu Yi, known as the "Iron Lady of the People's Republic of China," active in PRC politics through 2007,

retired in March 2008
- Eugenia Charles, the Prime Minister of Dominica from 1980 to 1995, known as the "Iron Lady of the Caribbean"
- Biljana Plavsic, the President and Vice-President of Republic of Srpska, and member of presidency of Socialist Republic of Bosnia and Herzegovina active from 1990-2000 is known as "The Serbian Iron Lady"
- Miriam Defensor Santiago, Tagged as the Iron Lady of the Philippines in the Philippine Senate
- Yulia Tymoshenko, Prime Minister of Ukraine from 2007 to 2010 (and in 2005)
- Dilma Rousseff, President of Brazil since 2011
- Angela Merkel, the Chancellor of Germany since 2005
- Ellen Johnson Sirleaf, the President of Liberia since 2006
- Dalia Grybauskaitė, the President of Lithuania since 2009
- Natalia Petkevich, First Deputy Head of the Administration of the President of Belarus since 2009

Politicians with similar names or variants

Some female politicians have been given similar nicknames:

- Neelie Kroes, the European Commissioner for Competition, referred to as the "Iron Lady of Antitrust" or "Steely Neelie"
- The Iron (or Steel) Butterfly is a nickname of former Philippine first lady Imelda Marcos.
- Iron Rita is a nickname of former Dutch immigration minister Rita Verdonk
- "Jern-Erna" (meaning; "Iron-Erna") is a nickname of the leader of the Norwegian Conservative Party, Erna Solberg.
- Former United States Secretary of State Madeleine Albright was given the nickname "Titanium Lady", playing on some of her similarities with Thatcher.
- In response to Manuela Ferreira Leite's nickname "Dama de Ferro Portuguesa" (Portuguese Iron Lady), her opponents and critics ironically started referring to her as "Dama de Latão" (Yellow brass Lady) and popularising the term.

Other uses

"The Iron Lady" ("*la dame de fer*") is a popular Parisian nickname for the Eiffel Tower.

"Iron Lady of the Seas", a 1984 video, and *Iron Lady at Sea*, a 1988 book, are about *Star of India*, the oldest iron-hulled merchant ship afloat launched in 1863.

Iron Lady is also the title of a song by Phil Ochs. In this song, the Iron Lady is a metaphor for the electric chair. This song was also performed by Diamanda Galás on her live album Malediction & Prayer in dedication to Aileen Wuornos.

Iron Lady is a Warcraft III LAN gaming competition held by SteelSeries and directed at female Chinese players. The event was created in 2007 and has completed 2 seasons already. Some well known players include Zhang 'Cang' Xiangliang and Xu "Sara" Yinghua, both of whom played in the IronLady.2 Final.

Iron Lady is the title of a 1980 comedy audio album lampooning UK Prime Minister Margaret Thatcher, written by satirist John Wells, featuring noted Thatcher impersonator Janet Brown, produced by Martin Lewis. The album consisted of skits and songs including a song also titled *Iron Lady*

The Iron Lady is the title of a 2011 film based on Margaret Thatcher, which is currently in pre-production.

Source (edited): "http://en.wikipedia.org/wiki/Iron_Lady"

Maggie Out

"**Maggie Out**" was a chant popular during the Miners' Strike, student grant protests, Poll Tax protests and other public demonstrations that fell within the time when Margaret Thatcher was the Prime Minister of the United Kingdom.

The chant called for her to be removed from that role. It was referred to, in that context, during a parliamentary session in 1984.

When Margaret Thatcher felt compelled to resign some people had memories of chanting it for thirteen years. People were passionate about this group activity and associated it with varied political struggles from that time.

It is a variant of the "Oggy Oggy Oggy, Oi Oi Oi" chant. When used in that format, the lyrics were:
Maggie, Maggie, Maggie!
Out! Out! Out!
Maggie, Maggie, Maggie!
Out! Out! Out!
Maggie!
Out!
Maggie!
Out!
Maggie, Maggie, Maggie!
Out! Out! Out!
The chorus of the chant became the title of a compilation album from Anagram Records (Catalog#:GRAM 28) released in 1987.

The Larks produced a track called "Maggie, Maggie, Maggie (Out, Out, Out)" which was included on the Miners' Benefit LP "Here We Go" on Sterile Records.

Comedian Alexei Sayle remarked humorously that he couldn't find his way around London unless he walked down the middle of the streets shouting the words.

Since 1990 two variants of this song have been heard - adapted for both her successors; replacing 'Major' for 'Maggie' during the tenure of John Major and 'Tony' for 'Maggie' since Tony Blair's plan for the Iraq War in 2003.

The song has occasionally been revived to "greet" Thatcher's public outings following her resignation as Prime Minister, but with the word "gone" substituted for "out".

Source (edited): "http://en.wikipedia.org/wiki/Maggie_Out"

Margaret Thatcher

Margaret Hilda Thatcher, Baroness Thatcher, LG, OM, PC, FRS (née **Roberts**; born 13 October 1925) is a former Prime Minister of the United Kingdom who served from 1979 to 1990.

Born in Grantham, Lincolnshire, Thatcher studied chemistry at Somerville College, Oxford before qualifying as a barrister. In the 1959 general election she became MP for Finchley. Edward Heath appointed Thatcher Secretary of State for Education and Science in his 1970 government. In 1975 she was elected Leader of the Conservative Party, the first woman to head a major UK political party, and in 1979 she became the UK's first female Prime Minister.

After entering 10 Downing Street Thatcher was determined to reverse what she perceived as a precipitous national decline. Her political philosophy and economic policies emphasised deregulation, particularly of the financial sector, flexible labour markets, the sale or closure of state-owned companies, and the withdrawal of subsidies to others. Thatcher's popularity waned amid recession and high unemployment, until economic recovery and the 1982 Falklands War brought a resurgence of support resulting in her re-election in 1983.

Thatcher survived an assassination attempt in 1984, and her hard line against trade unions and tough rhetoric in opposition to the Soviet Union earned her the nickname of the "Iron Lady". Thatcher was re-elected for a third term in 1987, but her Community Charge was widely unpopular and her views on the European Community were not shared by others in her Cabinet. She resigned as Prime Minister and party leader in November 1990 after Michael Heseltine's challenge to her leadership of the Conservative Party.

Thatcher holds a life peerage as Baroness Thatcher, of Kesteven in the County of Lincolnshire, which entitles her to sit in the House of Lords.

Early life and education

Margaret Thatcher's birthplace, in Grantham

Commemorative plaque on the building in which Margaret Thatcher was born

Margaret Roberts was born on 13 October 1925. Her father was Alfred Roberts, originally from Northamptonshire, and her mother was Beatrice Ethel (née Stephenson) from Lincolnshire. She spent her childhood in Grantham, where her father owned two grocery shops. She and her older sister Muriel were raised in the flat above the larger of the two, located near the railway line. Her father was active in local politics and religion, serving as an alderman and a Methodist lay preacher, and brought up his daughter as a strict Methodist. He came from a Liberal family but stood – as was then customary in local government – as an Independent. He lost his position as alderman in 1952 after the Labour Party won its first majority on Grantham Council in 1950.

Roberts attended Huntingtower Road Primary School and won a scholarship to Kesteven and Grantham Girls' School. Her school reports showed hard work and continual improvement; her extracurricular activities included the piano, field hockey, poetry recitals, swimming and walking. She was head girl in 1942–43. In her upper sixth year she applied for a scholarship to study chemistry at Somerville College, Oxford but was initially rejected, and only offered a place after another candidate withdrew. She arrived at Oxford in 1943 and graduated in 1947 with Second Class Honours in the four-year Chemistry Bachelor of Science degree; in her final year she specialised in crystallography under the supervision of Dorothy Hodgkin.

Roberts became President of the Oxford University Conservative Association in 1946. She was influenced at university by political works such as Friedrich von Hayek's *The Road to Serfdom* (1944), which condemned economic intervention by government as a precursor to an authoritarian state.

After graduating, Roberts moved to Colchester in Essex to work as a research chemist for BX Plastics. She joined the local Conservative Association and attended the party conference at Llandudno in 1948, as a representative of the University Graduate Conservative Association. One of her Oxford friends was also a friend of the Chair of the Dartford Conservative Association in Kent, who were looking for candidates. Officials of the association were so impressed by her that they asked her to apply, even though she was not on the Conservative party's approved list: she was selected in January 1951 and added to the approved list *post ante*. At a dinner following her formal adoption as Conservative candidate for Dartford in February 1951 she met Denis Thatcher, a successful and wealthy divorced businessman, who drove her to her Essex train. In preparation for the election Roberts moved to Dartford, where she supported herself by working as a research chemist for J. Lyons and Co. in Hammersmith, part of a team developing emulsifiers for ice cream.

Early political career

In the February 1950 and October 1951 general elections she campaigned for the safe Labour seat of Dartford, where she attracted media attention as the youngest and the only female candidate. She lost both times to Norman Dodds, but reduced the Labour majority by 6,000, and then a further 1,000. During the campaigns, she was supported by her parents and by Denis Thatcher, whom she married in December 1951. Denis funded his wife's studies for the bar; she qualified as a barrister in 1953 and specialised in taxation. That same year her twins, Carol and Mark, were born.

Member of Parliament (1959–1970)

Thatcher began looking for a safe Conservative seat in the mid-1950s. She was narrowly rejected as the candidate for Orpington in 1955, but was selected for Finchley in April 1958. She won the seat after a hard campaign in the 1959 election and was elected as a Member of Parliament (MP). Her maiden speech was in support of her private member's bill (Public Bodies (Admission to Meetings) Act 1960), requiring local authorities to hold their council meetings in public. In 1961 she went against the Conservative Party's official position by voting for the restoration of birching.

In October 1961 Thatcher was promoted to the front bench as Parliamentary Undersecretary at the Ministry of Pensions and National Insurance in Harold Macmillan's administration. After the loss of the 1964 election she became Conservative spokesman on Housing and Land, in which position she advocated her party's policy of allowing tenants to buy their council houses. She moved to the Shadow Treasury team in 1966, and as Treasury spokesman opposed Labour's mandatory price and income controls, arguing that they would produce contrary effects to those intended and distort the economy.

At the Conservative Party Conference of 1966 she criticised the high-tax policies of the Labour Government as being steps "not only towards Socialism, but towards Communism". She argued that lower taxes served as an incentive to hard work. Thatcher was one of the few Conservative MPs to support Leo Abse's Bill to decriminalise male homosexuality and voted in favour of David Steel's Bill to legalise abortion, as well as a ban on hare coursing. She supported the retention of capital punishment and voted against the relaxation of divorce laws.

In 1967 she was selected by the United States Embassy in London to take part in the International Visitor Leadership Program (then called the Foreign Leader Program), a professional exchange programme that gave her the opportunity to spend about six weeks visiting various US cities, political figures, and institutions such as the International Monetary Fund. Thatcher joined the Shadow Cabinet later that year as Shadow Fuel spokesman. Shortly before the 1970 general election, she was promoted to Shadow Transport, and then to Education.

Education Secretary (1970–1974)

The Conservative party under Edward Heath won the 1970 general election, and Thatcher was appointed Secretary of State for Education and Science. In her first months in office she attracted public attention as a result of the administration's attempts to cut spending. She gave priority to academic needs in schools, and imposed public expenditure cuts on the state education system, resulting in the abolition of free milk for schoolchildren aged seven to eleven. She held that few children would suffer if schools were charged for milk, but she agreed to provide younger children with a third of a pint daily, for nutritional purposes. Her decision provoked a storm of protest from the Labour party and the press, and led to the moniker "Margaret Thatcher, Milk Snatcher". Thatcher wrote in her autobiography: "I learned a valuable lesson [from the experience]. I had incurred the maximum of political odium for the minimum of political benefit."

Thatcher's term of office was marked by proposals for more local education authorities to close grammar schools and to adopt comprehensive secondary education. Although she was committed to a tiered secondary modern–grammar school system of education, and determined to preserve grammar schools, during her tenure as Education Secretary she turned down only 326 of 3,612 proposals for schools to become comprehensives; the proportion of pupils attending comprehensives rose from 32% to 62%.

Leader of the Opposition (1975–1979)

Margaret Thatcher, Leader of the Opposition, 18 September 1975

The Heath government continued to experience difficulties with oil embargoes and union demands for wage increases in 1973, and was defeated in the February 1974 general election. The Conservative result in the general election of October 1974 was even worse, and Thatcher mounted a challenge for the leadership of the party. Promising a fresh start, her main support came from the Conservative 1922 Committee. She defeated Heath on the first ballot and he resigned the leadership. In the second ballot she defeated Heath's preferred successor, William Whitelaw, and became party leader on 11 February 1975; she appointed Whitelaw as her deputy. Heath remained disenchanted with Thatcher to the end of his life for what he, and many of his supporters, perceived as her disloyalty in standing against him.

Thatcher began regularly to attend lunches at the Institute of Economic Affairs (IEA), a think tank founded by the poultry magnate Antony Fisher, a disciple of Friedrich von Hayek; she had been visiting the IEA and reading its publications since the early 1960s. There she was influenced by the ideas of Ralph Harris and Arthur Seldon, and she became the face of the ideological movement opposing the welfare state Keynesian economics they believed was weakening Britain. The institute's pamphlets proposed less government, lower taxes, and more freedom for business and consumers.

Thatcher began to work on her voice and screen image. The critic Clive James, writing in *The Observer* in 1977, compared her voice of 1973 to a cat sliding down a blackboard, but acknowledged her intelligence and mental agility.

On 19 January 1976 Thatcher made a speech in Kensington Town Hall in which she made a scathing attack on the Soviet Union:

The Russians are bent on world dominance, and they are rapidly acquiring the means to become the most powerful imperial nation the world has seen. The men in the Soviet *Politburo* do not have to worry about the ebb and flow of public opinion. They put guns before butter, while we put just about everything before guns.

In response, the Soviet Defence Ministry newspaper *Krasnaya Zvezda* (*Red Star*) gave her the nickname "Iron Lady". She took delight in the name, and it soon became associated with her image.

Despite an economic recovery in the late 1970s, the Labour government faced public unease about the direction of the country and a damaging series of strikes during the winter of 1978–79, popularly dubbed the "Winter of Discontent". The Conservatives attacked the Labour government's unemployment record, using advertising with the slogan *Labour Isn't Working*. A general election was called after James Callaghan's government lost a motion of no confidence in early 1979. The Conservatives won a 44-seat majority in the House of Commons, and Margaret Thatcher became the UK's first female Prime Minister.

Prime Minister (1979–1990)

Thatcher's Ministry meets with Reagan's Cabinet at the White House, 1981

Thatcher became Prime Minister on 4 May 1979. Arriving at 10 Downing Street, she said, in a paraphrase of the "Prayer of Saint Francis":
Where there is discord, may we bring harmony. Where there is error, may we bring truth. Where there is doubt, may we bring faith. And where there is despair, may we bring hope.

Domestic affairs

Thatcher was Prime Minister at a time of great racial tension in Britain. Her standing in the polls rose by 11 percent after she said in a TV interview during campaigning for the 1979 election: "The moment a minority threatens to become a big one, people get frightened. The British character has done so much for democracy, for law, that if there is any fear that it might be swamped, people are going to react and be rather hostile to those coming in". She complained privately about Asian immigration in July 1979, in the context of restricting the number of Vietnamese boat people settling in the UK. Her stance on these issues was perceived as part of a rising racist public discourse, which scholars have defined as the "new racism," which Thatcher alledgedly exploited to take votes from the openly racist National Front.

As Prime Minister, Thatcher met weekly with Queen Elizabeth II to discuss government business, and their relationship came under close scrutiny. In July 1986 the *Sunday Times* reported claims attributed to the Queen's advisers of a "rift" between Buckingham Palace and Downing Street "over a wide range of domestic and international issues". The Palace issued an official denial, heading off speculation about a possible constitutional crisis. After Thatcher's retirement a senior Palace source again dismissed as "nonsense" the "stereotyped idea" that she had not got along with the Queen, or that they had fallen out over Thatcherite policies. Thatcher later wrote "... I always found the Queen's attitude towards the work of the Government absolutely correct. ... stories of clashes between 'two powerful women' were just too good not to make up."

Economy and taxation

Thatcher's economic policy was influenced by monetarist thinking and economists such as Milton Friedman and Friedrich von Hayek. Together with Chancellor of the Exchequer Geoffrey Howe, she lowered direct taxes on income and increased indirect taxes. She increased interest rates to slow the growth of the money supply and thereby lower inflation, introduced cash limits on public spending, and reduced expenditures on social services such as education and housing. Her cuts in higher education spending resulted in her being the first Oxford-educated post-war Prime Minister not to be awarded an honorary doctorate by the University of Oxford, after a 738 to 319 vote of the governing assembly and a student petition. Her new centrally funded City Technology Colleges did not enjoy much success, and the Funding Agency for Schools was set up to control expenditure by opening and closing schools; the Social Market Foundation, a right-wing think tank, described it as having "an extraordinary range of dictatorial powers".

Some Heathite Conservatives in the Cabinet, the so-called "wets", expressed doubt over Thatcher's policies. The 1981 riots in England resulted in the British media discussing the need for a policy U-turn. At the 1980 Conservative Party conference, Thatcher addressed the issue directly, with a speech written by the playwright Ronald Millar that included the lines: "You turn if you want to. The lady's not for turning!"

Thatcher's job approval rating fell to 23% by December 1980, lower than recorded for any previous Prime Minister. As the recession of the early 1980s deepened she increased taxes, despite concerns expressed in a statement signed by 364 leading economists issued towards the end of March 1981.

By 1982 the UK began to experience signs of economic recovery; inflation was down to 8.6% from a high of 18%, but unemployment was over 3 million for the first time since the 1930s. By 1983 overall economic growth was stronger and inflation and mortgage rates were at their lowest levels since 1970, although manufacturing output had dropped by 30% since 1978 and unemployment remained high, peaking at 3.3 million in 1984.

Throughout the 1980s revenue from the 90% tax on North Sea oil extraction was used as a short-term funding source to balance the economy and pay the costs of reform.

Thatcher reformed local government taxes by replacing domestic rates—a tax based on the nominal rental value of a home—with the Community Charge (or poll tax) in which the same amount was charged to each adult resident. The new tax was introduced in Scotland in 1989 and in England and Wales the following year, and proved to be among the most unpopular policies of her premiership. Public disquiet culminated in a 70,000-strong demonstration in London on 31 March 1990; the demonstration around Trafalgar Square deteriorated into the Poll Tax Riots, leaving 113 people injured and 340 under arrest. The Community Charge was abolished by her successor, John Major.

Foreign affairs

The Thatchers with the Reagans standing at the North Portico of the White House before a state dinner, 16 November 1988

Thatcher took office in the final decade of the Cold War and became closely aligned with the policies of United States President Ronald Reagan, based on their mutual distrust of Communism, although she strongly opposed Reagan's October 1983 invasion of Grenada. During her first year as Prime Minister she supported NATO's decision to deploy US nuclear cruise and Pershing missiles in Western Europe, and permitted the US to station more than 160 cruise missiles at RAF Greenham Common, starting on 14 November 1983 and triggering mass protests by the Campaign for Nuclear Disarmament. She bought the Trident nuclear missile submarine system from the US to replace Polaris, tripling the UK's nuclear forces at an eventual cost of more than £12 billion (at 1996–97 prices). Thatcher's preference for defence ties with the US was demonstrated in the Westland affair of January 1986, when she acted with colleagues to allow the struggling helicopter manufacturer Westland to refuse a takeover offer from the Italian firm Agusta in favour of the management's preferred option, a link with Sikorsky Aircraft Corporation. The UK Defence Secretary, Michael Heseltine, who had supported the Agusta deal, resigned in protest.

On 2 April 1982 the ruling military junta in Argentina ordered the invasion of the British Falkland Islands and South Georgia, triggering the Falklands War. The subsequent crisis was "a defining moment of her [Thatcher's] premiership". At the suggestion of Harold Macmillan and Robert Armstrong, she set up and chaired a small War Cabinet (formally called ODSA, Overseas and Defence committee, South Atlantic) to take charge of the conduct of the war, which by 5–6 April had authorised and despatched a naval task force to retake the islands. Argentina surrendered on 14 June and the operation was hailed a success, notwithstanding the deaths of 255 British servicemen and 3 Falkland Islanders. Argentinian deaths totalled 649, half of them after the nuclear-powered submarine HMS *Conqueror* torpedoed and sank the cruiser ARA *General Belgrano* on 2 May. Thatcher was criticised for the neglect of the Falklands' defence that led to the war, and notably by Tam Dalyell in parliament for the decision to sink the *Belgrano*, but overall she was considered a highly talented and committed war leader. The "Falklands factor", an economic recovery beginning early in 1982, and a bitterly divided Labour opposition contributed to Thatcher's second election victory in 1983.

Thatcher's antipathy towards European integration became more pronounced during her premiership, particularly after her third election victory in 1987. During a 1998 speech in Bruges she outlined her opposition to proposals from the European Community (EC), forerunner of the European Union, for a federal structure and increased centralisation of decision making. She had supported British membership of the EC, despite believing that the role of the organisation should be limited to ensuring free trade and effective competition, and feared that the EC's approach was at odds with her views on smaller government and deregulation; in 1988, she remarked, "We have not successfully rolled back the frontiers of the state in Britain, only to see them re-imposed at a European level, with a European super-state exercising a new dominance from Brussels". Thatcher was firmly opposed to the UK's membership of the Exchange Rate Mechanism, a precursor to European monetary union, believing that it would constrain the British economy, despite the urging of her Chancellor of the Exchequer Nigel Lawson and Foreign Secretary Geoffrey Howe, but she was persuaded by John Major to join in October 1990, at what proved to be too high a rate.

In April 1986 Thatcher permitted US F-111s to use Royal Air Force bases for the bombing of Libya in retaliation for the alleged Libyan bombing of a Berlin discothèque, citing the right of self-defence under Article 51 of the UN Charter. Polls suggested that less than one in three British citizens approved of Thatcher's decision. She was in the US on a state visit when Iraqi leader Saddam Hussein invaded neighbouring Kuwait in August 1990. During her talks with US President George H. W. Bush, who had succeeded Reagan in 1989, she recommended intervention, and put pressure on Bush to deploy troops in the Middle East to drive the Iraqi army out of Kuwait. Bush was somewhat apprehensive about the plan, prompting Thatcher to remark to him during a telephone conversation that "This was no time to go wobbly!" Thatcher's government provided military forces to the international coalition in the build-up to the Gulf War, but she had resigned by the time hostilities began on 17 January 1991.

Thatcher was one of the first Western leaders to respond warmly to reformist Soviet leader Mikhail Gorbachev. Following Reagan–Gorbachev summit meetings and reforms enacted by Gorbachev in the USSR, she declared in November 1988 that "We're not in a Cold War now", but rather in a "new relationship much wider than the Cold War ever was". She went on a state visit to the Soviet Union in 1984, and met with Gorbachev and Nikolai Ryzhkov, the Chairman of the Council of Ministers. Thatcher was initially opposed to German reunification, telling Gorbachev that it "would lead to a change to postwar borders, and we cannot allow that because such a development would undermine the stability of the whole international situation and could endanger our security". She expressed concern that a united Germany would align itself more closely with the Soviet Union and move away from NATO. In contrast she was an advocate of Croatian and Slovenian independence. In a 1991 interview for Croatian Radiotelevision, Thatcher commented on the Yugoslav Wars; she was critical of Western governments for not recognising the breakaway republics of Croatia and Slovenia as independent states and supplying them with arms after the Serbian-led Yugoslav Army attacked.

Industrial relations

Thatcher was committed to reducing the power of the trade unions, whose leadership she accused of undermining parliamentary democracy and economic performance through strike action. Several unions launched strikes in response to legislation introduced to curb their power, but resistance eventually collapsed. Only 39% of union members voted for Labour in the 1983 general election. According to the BBC, Thatcher "managed to destroy the power of the trade unions for almost a generation".

The miners' strike was the biggest confrontation between the unions and the Thatcher government. In March 1984 the National Coal Board (NCB) proposed to close 20 of the 174 state-owned mines and cut 20,000 jobs out of 187,000. Two-thirds of the country's miners, led by the National Union of Mineworkers (NUM) under Arthur Scargill, downed tools in protest. Thatcher refused to meet the union's demands and compared the miners' dispute to the Falklands conflict two years earlier, declaring in a speech in 1984: "We had to fight the enemy without in the Falklands. We always have to be aware of the enemy within, which is much more difficult to fight and more dangerous to liberty." After a year out on strike, in March 1985, the NUM leadership conceded without a deal. The cost to the economy was estimated to be at least £1.5 billion, and the strike was blamed for much of the pound's fall against the US dollar. The government closed 25 unprofitable coal mines in 1985, and by 1992 a total of 97 had been closed; those that remained were privatised in 1994. The eventual closure of 150 coal mines, not all of which were losing money, resulted in the loss of tens of thousands of jobs and devastated entire communities. Miners had helped bring down the Heath government, and Thatcher was determined to succeed where he had failed. Her strategy of preparing fuel stocks, appointing a union-busting NCB leader in Ian MacGregor, and ensuring police were adequately trained and equipped with riot gear, contributed to her victory.

The number of stoppages across the UK peaked at 4583 in 1979, when more than 29 million working days were lost. In 1984, the year of the miners' strike, there were 1221, resulting in the loss of more than 27 million working days. Stoppages then fell steadily throughout the rest of Thatcher's premiership; in 1990 there were 630 and fewer than 2 million working days lost, and they continued to fall thereafter. Trade union membership also fell, from 13.5 million in 1979 to less than 10 million by the time Thatcher left office in 1990.

Privatisation

The policy of privatisation has been called "a crucial ingredient of Thatcherism". After the 1983 election the sale of state utilities accelerated; more than £29 billion was raised from the sale of nationalised industries, and another £18 billion from the sale of council houses.

The process of privatisation, especially the preparation of nationalised industries for privatisation, was associated with marked improvements in performance, particularly in terms of labour productivity, although it is not clear how far this can be attributed to the merits of privatisation itself. Andrew Glyn, a Marxian economist, believed that the "productivity miracle" observed in British industry under Thatcher was achieved not so much by increasing the overall productivity of labour as by reducing workforces and increasing unemployment. A number of the privatised industries including gas, water, and electricity, were natural monopolies for which privatisation involved little increase in competition. The privatised industries that demonstrated improvement often did so while still under state ownership. British Steel, for instance, made great gains in profitability while still a nationalised industry under the government-appointed chairmanship of Ian MacGregor, who faced down trade-union opposition to close plants and reduce the workforce by half. Regulation was also significantly expanded to compensate for the loss of direct government control, with the foundation of regulatory bodies like Ofgas, Oftel and the National Rivers Authority. There was no clear pattern to the degree of competition, regulation, and performance among the privatised industries; in most cases privatisation benefitted consumers in terms of lower prices and improved efficiency, but the results overall were "mixed".

Thatcher always resisted rail privatisation, and was said to have told Transport Secretary Nicholas Ridley "Railway privatisation will be the Waterloo of this government. Please never mention the railways to me again." Shortly before her resignation, she accepted the arguments for privatising British Rail, which her successor John Major implemented in 1994. *The Economist* later considered the move to have been "a disaster".

The privatisation of public assets was combined with financial deregulation in an attempt to fuel economic growth. Geoffrey Howe abolished Britain's exchange controls in 1979, allowing more capital to be invested in foreign markets, and the Big Bang of 1986 removed many restrictions on the London Stock Exchange. The Thatcher government encouraged growth in the finance and service sectors to compensate for Britain's ailing manufacturing industry. Political economist Susan Strange called this new financial growth model "casino capitalism", reflecting her view that speculation and financial trading were becoming more important to the economy than industry.

Northern Ireland

Campaign UK, 1987. Troubled Images Exhibition, Linen Hall Library, Belfast, August 2010

In 1981, Provisional Irish Republican Army (PIRA) and Irish National Liberation Army (INLA) prisoners in Northern Ireland's Maze Prison began a hunger strike in an effort to regain the status of political prisoners that had been removed five years earlier under the preceding Labour government. Bobby Sands began the strike, saying that he would fast until death unless prison inmates won concessions over their living conditions. Thatcher refused to countenance a return to political status for the prisoners, declaring "Crime is crime is crime; it is not political", but nevertheless the UK government privately contacted republican leaders in a bid to bring the hunger strikes to an end. After the deaths of Sands and nine others some rights were restored to paramilitary prisoners, but not official recognition of their political status. Violence in Northern Ireland escalated significantly during the hunger strikes; in 1982 Sinn Féin politician Danny Morrison described Thatcher as "the biggest bastard we have ever known".

Thatcher narrowly escaped injury in a PIRA assassination attempt at a Brighton hotel early in the morning of 12 October 1984. Five people were killed, including the wife of Cabinet Minister John Wakeham. Thatcher was staying at the hotel to attend the Conservative Party Conference, which she insisted should open as scheduled the following day. She delivered her speech as planned, a move that was widely supported across the political spectrum and enhanced her popularity with the public.

On 6 November 1981 Thatcher and Irish Taoiseach Garret FitzGerald had established the Anglo-Irish Inter-Governmental Council, a forum for meetings between the two governments. On 15 November 1985, Thatcher and FitzGerald signed the Hillsborough Anglo-Irish Agreement, the first time a British government had given the Republic of Ireland an advisory role in the governance of Northern Ireland. In protest the Ulster Says No movement attracted 100,000 to a rally in Belfast, Ian Gow resigned as Minister of State in the HM Treasury, and all fifteen Unionist MPs resigned their parliamentary seats; only one was not returned in the subsequent by-elections on 23 January 1986.

Resignation

Thatcher in 1990

Thatcher was challenged for the leadership of the Conservative Party by virtually unknown backbench MP Sir Anthony Meyer in the 1989 leadership election. Of the 374 Conservative MPs eligible to vote 314 voted for Thatcher and 33 for Meyer. Her supporters in the party viewed the result as a success, and rejected suggestions that there was discontent within the party.

During her premiership Thatcher had

the second-lowest average approval rating, at 40 percent, of any post-war Prime Minister. Polls consistently showed that she was less popular than her party. A self-described conviction politician, Thatcher always insisted that she did not care about her poll ratings, pointing instead to her unbeaten election record.

Opinion polls in September 1990 reported that Labour had established a 14% lead over the Conservatives, and by November the Conservatives had been trailing Labour for 18 months. These ratings, together with Thatcher's combative personality and willingness to override colleagues' opinions, contributed to discontent within the Conservative party.

On 1 November 1990 Geoffrey Howe, the last remaining member of Thatcher's original 1979 cabinet, resigned from his position as Deputy Prime Minister over her refusal to agree to a timetable for Britain to join the European single currency. In his resignation speech on 13 November, Howe commented on Thatcher's European stance: "It is rather like sending your opening batsmen to the crease only for them to find the moment that the first balls are bowled that their bats have been broken before the game by the team captain." His resignation was fatal to Thatcher's premiership.

The next day, Michael Heseltine mounted a challenge for the leadership of the Conservative Party. Opinion polls had indicated that he would give the Conservatives a national lead over Labour. Although Thatcher won the first ballot, Heseltine attracted sufficient support (152 votes) to force a second ballot. Thatcher initially stated that she intended to "fight on and fight to win" the second ballot, but consultation with her Cabinet persuaded her to withdraw. After seeing the Queen, calling other world leaders, and making one final Commons speech, she left Downing Street in tears. She regarded her ousting as a betrayal.

Thatcher was replaced as Prime Minister and party leader by her Chancellor John Major, who oversaw an upturn in Conservative support in the 17 months leading up to the 1992 general election and led the Conservatives to their fourth successive victory on 9 April 1992. Thatcher favoured Major over Heseltine in the leadership contest, but her support for him weakened in later years.

Later years

Thatcher returned to the backbenches as MP for Finchley for two years after leaving the premiership. She retired from the House at the 1992 election, aged 66, saying that leaving the Commons would allow her more freedom to speak her mind.

Post-Commons

After leaving the House of Commons, Thatcher became the first former Prime Minister to set up a foundation; it closed down in 2005 because of financial difficulties. She wrote two volumes of memoirs, *The Downing Street Years* (1993) and *The Path to Power* (1995).

In July 1992 Thatcher was hired by the tobacco company Philip Morris as a "geopolitical consultant" for $250,000 per year and an annual contribution of $250,000 to her foundation. She also earned $50,000 for each speech she delivered.

In August 1992 Thatcher called for NATO to stop the Serbian assault on Goražde and Sarajevo to end ethnic cleansing during the Bosnian War. She compared the situation in Bosnia to "the worst excesses of the Nazis", and warned that there could be a "holocaust". She made a series of speeches in the Lords criticising the Maastricht Treaty, describing it as "a treaty too far" and stated "I could never have signed this treaty". She cited A. V. Dicey when stating that as all three main parties were in favour of revisiting the treaty, the people should have their say.

Thatcher with Mikhail Gorbachev (left) and Brian Mulroney (centre) at Reagan's funeral.

Thatcher was honorary Chancellor of the College of William and Mary in Virginia (1993–2000) and also of the University of Buckingham (1992–1999), the UK's first private university, which she had opened in 1975.

After Tony Blair's election as Labour Party leader in 1994, Thatcher praised Blair in an interview as "probably the most formidable Labour leader since Hugh Gaitskell. I see a lot of socialism behind their front bench, but not in Mr Blair. I think he genuinely has moved."

In 1998 Thatcher called for the release of former Chilean dictator Augusto Pinochet when Spain had him arrested and sought to try him for human rights violations, citing the help he gave Britain during the Falklands War. In 1999 she visited him while he was under house arrest near London. Pinochet was released in March 2000 on medical grounds by the Home Secretary Jack Straw, without facing trial.

In the 2001 general election Thatcher supported the Conservative general election campaign, but did not endorse Iain Duncan Smith as she had done for John Major and William Hague. In the Conservative leadership election shortly after, she supported Smith over Kenneth Clarke.

In March 2002 Thatcher's book *Statecraft: Strategies for a Changing World*, dedicated to Ronald Reagan, was released. In it, she claimed there would be no peace in the Middle East until Saddam Hussein was toppled, that Israel must trade land for peace, and that the European Union (EU) was "fundamentally unreformable", "a classic utopian project, a monument to the vanity of intellectuals, a programme whose inevitable destiny is failure". She argued that Britain should renegotiate its terms of membership or else leave the EU and join the North American Free Trade Area. The book was serialised in *The Times* on 18 March; on 23 March she announced that on the advice of her doctors she would cancel all planned speaking engagements and accept no more.

Since 2003

Sir Denis Thatcher died on 26 June 2003 and was cremated on 3 July. She had paid tribute to him in *The Downing Street Years*, writing "Being Prime Minister is a lonely job. In a sense, it ought to be: you cannot lead from the crowd. But with Denis there I was never alone. What a man. What a husband. What a friend".

On 11 June 2004 Thatcher attended the state funeral service for Ronald Reagan. She delivered her eulogy via videotape; in view of her health, the message had been pre-recorded several months earlier. Thatcher then flew to California with the Reagan entourage, and attended the memorial service and interment ceremony for the president at the Ronald Reagan Presidential Library.

Thatcher attends the Washington memorial service marking the 5th anniversary of the 11 September 2001 attacks, pictured with Dick Cheney and his wife

Thatcher celebrated her 80th birthday at the Mandarin Oriental Hotel in Hyde Park, London, on 13 October 2005, at which the guests included the Queen, The Duke of Edinburgh, Princess Alexandra and Tony Blair. Geoffrey Howe, by then Lord Howe of Aberavon, was also present, and said of his former leader: "Her real triumph was to have transformed not just one party but two, so that when Labour did eventually return, the great bulk of Thatcherism was accepted as irreversible."

In 2006 Thatcher attended the official Washington, D.C. memorial service to commemorate the fifth anniversary of the 11 September 2001 attacks on the United States. She was a guest of the Vice President, Dick Cheney, and met with Secretary of State Condoleezza Rice during her visit.

In February 2007 Thatcher became the first living UK Prime Minister to be honoured with a statue in the Houses of Parliament. The bronze statue stands opposite that of her political hero, Sir Winston Churchill, and was unveiled on 21 February 2007 with Thatcher in attendance; she made a rare and brief speech in the members' lobby of the House of Commons, responding: "I might have preferred iron – but bronze will do ... It won't rust." The statue shows her addressing the House of Commons, with her right arm outstretched.

Thatcher returned to 10 Downing Street in late November 2009 for the unveiling of an official portrait by the artist Richard Stone, an unusual honour for a living ex-Prime Minister. Stone had previously painted portraits of the Queen and the Queen Mother.

Thatcher suffered several small strokes in 2002 and was advised by her doctors not to engage in any more public speaking. After collapsing at a House of Lords dinner, she was admitted to St Thomas' Hospital in central London on 7 March 2008 for tests. Her daughter Carol has recounted ongoing memory loss.

At the Conservative Party conference in 2010, the new Prime Minister David Cameron announced that he would invite Thatcher back to 10 Downing Street on her 85th birthday for a party to be attended by past and present ministers. She pulled out of the celebration because of flu. She was invited to the Royal Wedding on 29 April 2011 but did not attend, reportedly due to ill health.

Thatcher remains identified with her remarks to the reporter Douglas Keay, for *Woman's Own* magazine in September 1987:

I think we have gone through a period when too many children and people have been given to understand "I have a problem, it is the Government's job to cope with it!" or "I have a problem, I will go and get a grant to cope with it!" "I am homeless, the Government must house me!" and so they are casting their problems on society and who is society? There is no such thing! There are individual men and women and there are families and no government can do anything except through people and people look to themselves first. It is our duty to look after ourselves and then also to help look after our neighbour and life is a reciprocal business and people have got the entitlements too much in mind without the obligations.

To her supporters, Margaret Thatcher remains a figure who revitalised Britain's economy, impacted the trade unions, and re-established the nation as a world power. She oversaw an increase from 7% to 25% of adults owning shares, and more than a million families bought their council houses, giving an increase from 55% to 67% in owner-occupiers. Total personal wealth rose by 80%. Victory in the Falklands conflict and her strong alliance with the United States are also remembered as some of her greatest achievements.

Thatcher's premiership was also marked by high unemployment and social unrest, and many critics fault her economic policies for the unemployment level; many of the areas affected by high unemployment as a result of her monetarist economic policieshave still not fully recovered and are also blighted by social problems including drug abuse and family breakdown. Speaking in Scotland in April 2009, before the 30th anniversary of her election as Prime Minister, Thatcher insisted she had no regrets, and was right to introduce the poll tax and to remove subsidies from "outdated industries, whose markets were in terminal decline" which had created "the culture of dependency, which had done such damage to Britain".

Thatcher often referred after the war to the "Falklands Spirit"; Hastings and Jenkins (1983) suggested that this reflected her preference for the streamlined decision-making of her War Cabinet over the painstaking deal-making of peace-time cabinet government.

Critics have regretted Thatcher's influence in the abandonment of full employment, poverty reduction and a consensual civility as bedrock policy objectives. Many recent biographers have been critical of aspects of the Thatcher years and Michael White, writing in *New Statesman* in February 2009, challenged the view that her reforms had brought a net benefit. Despite being Britain's first woman Prime Minister, some critics contend Thatcher did "little to advance the political cause of women", either within her party or the government, and some British feminists regarded her as "an enemy".

The term "Thatcherism" came to refer to her policies as well as aspects of her ethical outlook and personal style, including moral absolutism, nationalism, interest in the individual, and an uncompromising approach to achieving political goals. Influenced at the outset by Keith Joseph, Thatcherism remains a potent byword in British political parlance, with both Tony Blair and Gordon Brown defining policies in post-Thatcherite terms, and David Cameron saying after a dinner with Thatcher in February 2009: "You have got to do the right thing even if it is painful. Don't trim or track all over the place. Set your course and take the difficult decisions because that is what needs to be done ... I think that influence, that character she had, that conviction she had, I think that will be very important."

Thatcher's tenure of 11 years and 209 days as Prime Minister was the longest since Lord Salisbury (13 years and 252 days in three spells starting in 1885), and the longest continuous period in office since Lord Liverpool (14 years and 305 days starting in 1812).

Honours

US President George H. W. Bush awards Thatcher the Presidential Medal of Freedom, 1991

Thatcher became a Privy Councillor (PC) upon becoming Secretary of State for Education and Science in 1970. She was appointed a Member of the Order of Merit (OM) (an order within the personal gift of the Queen) within two weeks of leaving office. Denis Thatcher was made a Baronet at the same time. She became a peer in the House of Lords in 1992 with a life peerage as Baroness Thatcher of Kesteven in the County of Lincolnshire. She was appointed a Lady Companion of the Order of the Garter, the UK's highest order of chivalry, in 1995.

She was elected as a Fellow of the Royal Society (FRS) in 1983, and was the first woman entitled to full membership rights as an honorary member of the Carlton Club on becoming leader of the Conservative Party in 1975.

In the Falkland Islands, Margaret Thatcher Day has been marked every 10 January since 1992, commemorating her visit in 1983. Thatcher Drive in Stanley is named for her, as is Thatcher Peninsula in South Georgia, where the task force troops first set foot on the Falklands.

Thatcher has been awarded the Presidential Medal of Freedom, the highest civilian honour awarded by the US; the Republican Senatorial Medal of Freedom; and the Ronald Reagan Freedom Award. She is a patron of the Heritage Foundation, which established the Margaret Thatcher Center for Freedom in 2005. Speaking of Heritage president Ed Feulner, at the first Clare Booth Luce lecture in September 1993, Thatcher said: "You didn't just advise President Reagan on what he should do; you told him how he could do it. And as a practising politician I can testify that that is the only advice worth having."

Other awards include Dame Grand Cross of the Croatian Grand Order of King Dmitar Zvonimir.

Media depictions

Depictions of Margaret Thatcher have featured in a number of television programmes, documentaries, films and plays; she was played by Patricia Hodge in Ian Curteis's long unproduced *The Falklands Play* (2002) and Lindsay Duncan in *Margaret* (2009). She was portrayed by Andrea Riseborough in the TV film *The Long Walk to Finchley*. Thatcher will be played by Meryl Streep in a film *The Iron Lady* (being filmed as at February 2011). She was also the inspiration for a number of protest songs.

Thatcher was lampooned by satirist John Wells in several media. Wells collaborated with Richard Ingrams on the spoof "Dear Bill" letters which ran as a column in *Private Eye* magazine, were published in book form, and were then adapted into a West End stage revue as *Anyone for Denis?*, starring Wells as Denis Thatcher. The stage show was followed by a 1982 TV special directed by Dick Clement. In 1979, Wells was commissioned by comedy producer Martin Lewis to write and perform on a comedy record album titled *Iron Lady: The Coming Of The Leader* on which Thatcher was portrayed by comedienne and noted Thatcher impersonator Janet Brown. The album consisted of skits and songs satirising Thatcher's rise to power.

Janet Brown's portrayals of Thatcher also included an appearance in the 1981 James Bond film For Your Eyes Only.

Anna Massey portrayed Thatcher in *Pinochet in Suburbia* (2002), which told the story of Chilean dictator Augusto Pinochet's house arrest in Britain during the late 1990s, and co-starred Derek Jacobi as Pinochet.

Also in 2002, Patricia Hodge portrayed Thatcher in *The Falklands Play*, centred on events during the Falklands conflict.

In 1989, when Thatcher was still in office, Maureen Lipman portrayed her in *About Face*, in which she and her husband (portrayed by John Wells) were kidnapped while on holiday.

In 1991, the year after Thatcher's resignation, Sylvia Syms portrayed her in the ITV special *Thatcher: The Final Days*, which was centred on the events which resulted in her fall from power.

Paula Wilcox portrayed Thatcher in the 2010 Jonathan Harvey play *Canary*, which was centred on the AIDS crisis of the mid 1980s.

Hilary Turner portrayed Thatcher in *First Among Equals*, a 1986 ITV adapation of the Jeffrey Archer novel.

Source (edited): "http://en.wikipedia.org/wiki/Margaret_Thatcher"

Mark Thatcher

The Honourable **Sir Mark Thatcher, 2nd Baronet** (born 15 August 1953) is the son of Sir Denis Thatcher and Baroness Thatcher, the former British Prime Minister, and twin brother of Carol Thatcher. In addition to his prominence as the son of one of the world's best known politicians, Thatcher has attracted headlines for his early youthful playboy lifestyle, involvement in motorsports, business associations, and for the role he played in an attempted coup in Equatorial Guinea, for which role he was fined three million rand (approximately $500,000) and received a four-year suspended jail sentence.

Personal life

Thatcher married Diane Burgdorf, the conservative Lutheran daughter of the millionaire Texas car dealer Theodore C. Burgdorf, on 14 February 1987 in Queen's Chapel of the Savoy, London, England. They reportedly met at a party for *D Magazine*, a Dallas lifestyle publication, while Thatcher was living in Texas as a representative of the luxury automotive company Lotus Cars. The family moved to South Africa, possibly to avoid bad publicity because of allegations against Mark Thatcher of racketeering that resulted in a £4 million civil action in 1994. They have a son (who is heir apparent to the baronetcy) and a daughter:
- Michael Thatcher (born 28 February 1989)
- Amanda Margaret Thatcher (born 1993)

On 19 September 2005, the couple announced their intention to divorce. Burgdorf married American statistician and sports card millionaire James Beckett in 2008.

In March 2008, Tim Walker revealed in the *Sunday Telegraph's* Mandrake diary that Thatcher had secretly married Lady Francis Russell (Sarah Jane Russell). She is the ex-wife of Lord Francis Russell (a younger son of John Russell, 13th Duke of Bedford), the daughter of Terence J. Clemence and a sister of The Viscountess Rothermere. During his marriage to Burgdorf, Thatcher had had an affair with Russell, about which Burgdorf had confronted her.

In 1982, while competing in the Paris-Dakar rally, Thatcher, his French co-driver, Anne-Charlotte Verney, and their mechanic went missing in the Sahara Desert for six days. On 9 January 1982, the trio became separated from a convoy of vehicles after they stopped to make repairs to a faulty steering arm. They were declared missing on 12 January; after a large-scale search, a C-130 Hercules search plane from the Algerian military spotted the white Peugeot 504 some 50 km off course on 14 January. Thatcher, Verney and the mechanic were all unharmed.

Thatcher also competed, with little success but less notoriety, on the circuits in Sports 2000, Thundersports and eventually graduated to the European Touring Car Championship with semi-works BMWs.

Business life

Thatcher was later employed in the jewellery business. His business dealings at the time that his mother was the Prime Minister were the subject of much press attention.

In 1998 South African authorities investigated his firm for running loan shark operations. A company owned by Thatcher offered unofficial small loans to hundreds of police officers, military personnel and civil servants. When they defaulted on the loans they were pursued by debt collectors and charged 20% interest rates, according to the Star of Johannesburg.

Other widely reported Thatcher embarrassments include allegations of U.S. tax evasion (a criminal case was eventually dropped) and a racketeering case in Texas which was settled out of court. According to *The Daily Telegraph* of 26 August 2004, "In 1998, he was at the centre of a scandal after he lent huge sums of money at exorbitant interest rates to more than 900 local police officers and civil servants in Cape Town. He admitted lending the cash but insisted that he had done nothing wrong. He is also thought to have profited from contracts to supply aviation fuel in various African countries."

The *Sunday Times*, quoting "city sources", said he had amassed a personal fortune of £60m, the majority of which is in offshore accounts, attributed to shrewd investments and a series of "astute deals in Africa".

Equatorial Guinea coup

On 25 August 2004, Thatcher was arrested at home in Constantia, Cape Town, South Africa. He was charged later that day with contravening two sections of South Africa's "Foreign Military Assistance Act", which bans South African residents from taking part in any foreign military activity. The charges related to "possible funding and logistical assistance in relation to [an] attempted coup in Equatorial Guinea" organized by Thatcher's friend, Simon Mann. He was released on bail of 2 million rand and spent a period of time under house arrest, but was bailed to London to live with his widowed mother while his wife and children moved to the family's home in Dallas, Texas.

On 24 November 2004, the Cape Town High Court upheld a subpoena from the South African Justice Ministry that required him to answer under oath questions from Equatorial Guinean authorities regarding the alleged coup attempt. He was due to face questioning on 25 November 2004, regarding offences under the South African Foreign Military Assistance Act; however, these proceedings were later postponed until 8 April 2005. Ultimately, following a process of plea bargaining, Thatcher pleaded guilty to negligence in investing in an aircraft "without taking proper investigations into what it would be used for". Thatcher admitted in court that he had paid the money, but said he was under the impression it was going to be invested in an air ambulance service to help the impoverished of Africa. This explanation was not believed by the judge and he was fined three million rand (approximately $500,000) and received a four-year suspended jail sentence.

On 3 April 2005, Thatcher, then living with his mother in Belgravia, London announced that his family home would be in Europe after he was refused a residence visa to live in the United States as a result of his guilty plea in the Equatorial Guinea affair. His children, he stated, will be educated in the United States.

Under the headline "Mark Thatcher — undesirable in Monaco?" French newspaper *Le Figaro* reported on 20 December 2005:
"Margaret Thatcher's son, the former British prime minister's nefarious offspring, will not be installing himself in the principality of Monaco as he hoped." A spokesman for Prince Albert II of Monaco told *Le Figaro* that Thatcher's residency card would not be renewed. "He has a temporary residency card valid for one year. It will not be renewed when it expires in the second half of 2006 and he will have to leave." The spokesman, Armand Deus, added: "I cannot say why it will not be renewed. But the Prince made things very clear during his investiture in July when he said that ethics will be at the centre of life in Monaco."
In Equatorial Guinea in June 2008, Simon Mann claimed during his trial testimony that Thatcher, now resident in Spain, "was not just an investor, he came completely on board and became a part of the management team" of the coup plot.

Titles and styles

Thatcher is entitled the usage of the pre-nominal style 'The Honourable' following the elevation of his mother, Margaret Thatcher, to the peerage as a baroness in 1992; he shares this courtesy with his twin sister, The Hon. Carol Thatcher. He inherited the Thatcher baronetcy on the death of his father, Sir Denis, in 2003. The baronetcy, created in 1991 for Sir Denis, was the first (and so far only) baronetcy created since 1964. It was not the first honour to be granted to a spouse of a British Prime Minister: the wives of both Benjamin Disraeli and Sir Winston Churchill were made peeresses in their own right, although the former excited controversy at the time.

Timeline of titles

- Mark Thatcher Esq. (15 August 1953–26 June 1992)
- *The Hon.* Mark Thatcher (26 June 1992 –26 June 2003)
- *The Hon.* Sir Mark Thatcher, 2nd Bt (26 June 2003–)

Source (edited): "http://en.wikipedia.org/wiki/Mark_Thatcher"

Premiership of Margaret Thatcher

The **Premiership of Margaret Thatcher** began on 4 May 1979, with a mandate to reverse the UK's economic decline and to reduce the role of the state in the economy. Margaret Thatcher was incensed by one contemporary view within the Civil Service, that its job was to manage the UK's decline from the days of Empire, and she wanted the country to assert a higher level of influence and leadership in international affairs. She was a philosophic soulmate of Ronald Reagan, elected in 1980 in the United States, and to a lesser extent Brian Mulroney, who was elected in 1984 in Canada. Free market conservatism now became the new dominant political philosophy in many western nations, dubbed neoliberalism. Indeed after years of socialist political dominance, Thatcher would go on to radically transform Britain more so than any leader of Britain since Clement Attlee, rejuvenating a stagnant world power but socially dividing much of the population.

First government 1979–1983

Deflationary strategy

Under the Thatcher government the taming of inflation displaced high employment as the primary policy objective.

As a monetarist, Thatcher started out in her economic policy by increasing interest rates to slow the growth of the money supply and thus lower inflation. She had a preference for indirect taxation over taxes on income, and value added tax (VAT) was raised sharply to 15%, with a resultant actual short-term rise in inflation. The fiscal and monetary squeeze, combined with the North Sea oil effect, appreciated the real exchange rate. These moves hit businesses—especially the manufacturing sector—and unemployment quickly passed two million, doubling the one million unemployed under the previous Labour government.

Political commentators harked back to the Heath Government's "U-turn" and speculated that Thatcher would follow suit, but she repudiated this approach at the 1980 Conservative party conference, telling the party: "To those waiting with bated breath for that favourite media catch-phrase—the U-turn—I have only one thing to say: you turn if you want to; the Lady's not for turning." That she meant what she said was confirmed in the 1981 budget, when, despite concerns expressed in an open letter from 364 leading economists, taxes were increased in the middle of a recession, leading to newspaper headlines the following morning of "Howe it Hurts", a reference to the Chancellor Geoffrey Howe.

In 1981, as unemployment soared and the government's popularity plunged, the party chairman, Lord Thorneycroft, and two cabinet ministers, Lord Carrington and Humphrey Atkins, confronted the prime minister and suggested she should resign; according to her adviser, Tim Bell, "Margaret just told them to go away". Thatcher's key ally in the party was home secretary and later deputy prime minister William Whitelaw. His moral authority and support allowed her to resist the internal threat from the Heathite wets.

After the 1981 Brixton riot, Employment Secretary Norman Tebbit, responding to a suggestion that rioting was caused by unemployment, observed that the unemployment of the 1930s was far worse than that of the 1980s—and that his father's generation never reacted by rioting. 'I grew up in the 1930s with an unemployed father,' Tebbit said. 'He did not riot. He got on his bike and looked for work, and he went on looking until he found it.'

Over two million manufacturing jobs were ultimately lost in the recession of 1979-81. This labour-shedding helped firms deal with long-standing X-inefficiency from over-manning, enabling the British economy to catch up to the productivity levels of other advanced capitalist countries.

The link between the money supply and inflation was proven accurate and by January 1982, the inflation rate had dropped back to 8.6% from earlier highs of 18%. Interest rates were then allowed to fall. Unemployment continued to rise, reaching an official figure of 3.6 million—although the criteria for defining who was unemployed were amended allowing some to estimate that unemployment in fact hit 5 million. However, Tebbit later suggested that, due to the high number of people claiming unemployment benefit while working, unemployment never reached three million.

By 1983, manufacturing output had dropped by 30% from 1978. The productivity turnaround from labour-shedding proved to be a one-off, and was not matched by growth in output. The industrial base was so reduced that thereafter the balance of payments in manufactured goods was in deficit. In 1983 Chancellor of the Exchequer Nigel Lawson told the House of Lords Select Committee on Overseas Trade:

There is no adamantine law that says we have to produce as much in the way of manufactures as we consume. If it does turn out that we are relatively more efficient in world terms at providing services than at producing goods, then our national interest lies in a surplus on services and a deficit on goods.

Iranian embassy siege

Thatcher's determination to face down political violence was first demonstrated during the 1980 siege of the Iranian embassy in Princes Gate, London, when for the first time in 70 years the armed forces were authorised to use lethal force on the British mainland. 26 hostages were held by six gunmen for six days in May, until the siege came to a dramatic end with a successful raid by SAS commandos. Later that day, 'Thatcher went to congratulate the SAS men involved and sat among them watching a re-run of the attack'. The breaking of the siege by the SAS was later celebrated by the public as one of television's greatest moments.

The appearance of decisiveness—christened the 'resolute approach' by the prime minister herself—became Thatcher's trademark, and a source of her popularity. In the words of one historian: 'The mood reflected Mrs Thatcher's Iron Lady stance, her proclaimed intention of laying the "Suez Syndrome" to rest and again projecting Britain as a great power. Celebration of the SAS was a key component in the popular militarism of the 1980s, fuelled by the continuing "war" against international terrorism and by the Falklands conflict and Gulf War. The storming of the Iranian Embassy had shown that Britain could meet terror with counter-terror: Mrs Thatcher's black-clad "terminators" would protect us.'

Commenting on the SAS's action, social services secretary Norman Fowler agreed: 'Mrs. Thatcher attracted public support because she seemed to be taking action which the public overwhelmingly thought was right but never thought any government would have the nerve to carry out.'

Northern Ireland

In May 1980, one day before Thatcher was due to meet the Irish Taoiseach, Charles Haughey, to discuss Northern Ireland, she announced in the House of Commons of the United Kingdom that "the future of the constitutional affairs of Northern Ireland is a matter for the people of Northern Ireland, this government, this parliament, *and no-one else.*"

In 1981, a number of Provisional Irish Republican Army (IRA) and Irish National Liberation Army prisoners in Northern Ireland's Maze Prison (known in Northern Ireland as 'Long Kesh', its previous official name) went on hunger strike to regain the status of political prisoners, which had been revoked five years earlier under the preceding Labour government. Bobby Sands, the first of the strikers, was elected as a Member of Parliament (MP) for the constituency of Fermanagh and South Tyrone a few weeks before he died.

Thatcher refused to countenance a return to political status for republican prisoners, famously declaring, 'Crime is crime is crime; it is not political.' After nine more men had starved themselves to death and the strike had ended, some rights were restored to paramilitary prisoners, but official recognition of their political status was not granted. Thatcher later asserted, 'The outcome was a significant defeat for the IRA.'

Thatcher also continued the policy of 'Ulsterisation' of the previous Labour government and its Secretary of State for Northern Ireland, Roy Mason, believing that the Unionists of Northern Ireland should be at the forefront in combating Irish republicanism. This meant relieving the burden on the mainstream British army and elevating the role of the Ulster Defence Regiment and the Royal Ulster Constabulary.

The Falklands

On 2 April 1982, a ruling military junta in Argentina invaded the Falkland Islands and South Georgia, a British overseas territory that Argentina had claimed since an 1810 dispute on the British settlement. The following day, Thatcher sent a naval task force to back diplomatic efforts with the threat of the use of force, and if negotiations failed, to recapture the islands and eject the invaders. The conflict escalated from there, evolving into an amphibious and ground combat operation. An opinion poll published prior to the British landing showed 70% support for military action. Argentina surrendered on 14 June and the operation was deemed a success, despite 258 British casualties. Victory brought a wave of patriotic enthusiasm and increased support for the Thatcher government, with *Newsweek* declaring "The Empire Strikes Back". One poll suggested that 84% of the electorate approved of the prime minister's handling of the crisis.

1983 General election

The 'Falklands Factor', along the resumption of economic growth by the end of 1982, bolstered the government's popularity. The Labour party at this time had split, and there was a new challenge in the SDP-Liberal Alliance, formed by an electoral pact between the Social Democratic Party and the Liberal Party. However, this grouping failed to make its intended breakthrough, despite briefly holding an opinion poll lead.

In the June 1983 general election, the Conservatives won 42.4% of the vote, the Labour party 27.6% and the Alliance 25.4% of the vote (though the gap between Labour and the Alliance was narrow in terms of votes, the Alliance attained only a fraction of the seats that Labour held).

Although the Conservatives' share of the vote had fallen slightly (1.5%) since 1979, Labour's vote had fallen by far more (9.3%) and in Britain's first past the post system, the Conservatives won a landslide victory. Under Margaret Thatcher, the Conservatives now had an overall majority of 144 MPs.

Second government 1983–1987

Industrial relations

Thatcher was committed to reducing the power of the trades unions but, unlike the Heath government, adopted a strategy of incremental change rather than a single Act. Several unions launched strikes in response, but these actions eventually collapsed. Gradually, Thatcher's reforms reduced the power and influence of the unions. The changes were chiefly focused upon preventing the recurrence of the large-scale industrial actions of the 1970s, but were also intended to ensure that the consequences for the participants would be severe if any future action was taken. The reforms were also aimed, Thatcher claimed, to democratise the unions, and return power to the members. The most significant measures were to make secondary industrial action illegal, to force union leadership to first win a ballot of the union membership before calling a strike, and to abolish the closed shop. Further laws banned workplace ballots and imposed postal ballots.

Miners' strike

Thatcher was a staunch opponent of Britain's powerful trade unions, leading her to many battles, most notably with the miners.

The National Coal Board received the largest amount of public subsidies going to any nationalised industry: by 1984 the annual cost to taxpayers of uneconomic pits had reached £1 billion. The year-long confrontation over strikes carried out from April 1984 by the National Union of Mineworkers (NUM), in opposition to proposals to close a large number of unprofitable mines, proved decisive. The government had made preparations to counter a strike by the NUM long in advance by building up coal stocks, ensuring that cuts in the electricity supply—the legacy of the industrial disputes of 1972—would not be repeated.

Police tactics during the strikes came under criticism from civil libertarians, but the images of crowds of militant miners attempting to prevent other miners from working proved a shock even to some supporters of the strikes. The mounting desperation and poverty of the striking families led to divisions within the regional NUM branches, and a breakaway union, the Union of Democratic Mineworkers (UDM), was soon formed. A group of workers, resigned to the impending failure of the actions and worn down by months of protests, began to defy the Union's rulings, starting splinter groups and advising workers that returning to work was the only viable option.

The miners' strike lasted a full year before the NUM leadership conceded without a deal. Conservative governments proceeded to close all but 15 of the country's pits, with the remaining 15 being sold off and privatised in 1994. Private companies have since then acquired licences to open new pits and open-cast sites, with the majority of the original mines destroyed and the land redeveloped.

The defeat of the miners' strike led to a long period of demoralisation in the whole of the trade union movement. Nigel Lawson, then chancellor of the exchequer, later recalled:

" The miners' strike was the central political event of the second Thatcher Administration. Just as the victory in the Falklands War exorcized the humiliation of Suez, so the eventual defeat of the NUM " etched in the public mind the end of militant trade unionism which had wrecked the economy and twice played a major part in driving elected governments from office.

Apartheid

The Thatcher government opposed the apartheid policy of the white-minority government of South Africa, but resisted international pressure to impose economic sanctions on the former colony, where the United Kingdom was the biggest foreign investor and principal trading partner.

At the end of March 1984, four South Africans were arrested in Coventry, remanded in custody, and charged with contravening the UN arms embargo, which prohibited exports to South Africa of military equipment. Thatcher took a personal interest in the Coventry Four, and 10 Downing Street requested daily summaries of the case from the prosecuting authority, HM Customs and Excise. Within a month, the Coventry Four had been freed from jail and allowed to travel to South Africa, on condition that they returned to England for their trial later that year. However in August 1984 South African foreign minister Pik Botha decided not to allow the Coventry Four to return to stand trial, forfeiting £200,000 bail money put up by the South African embassy in London.

In April 1984, Thatcher sent senior British diplomat, Sir John Leahy, to negotiate the release of 16 Britons who had been taken hostage by the Angolan rebel leader, Jonas Savimbi. At the time, Savimbi's UNITA guerrilla movement was financed and supported militarily by the apartheid regime of South Africa. On April 26, 1984 Leahy succeeded in securing the release of the British hostages at the UNITA base in Jamba, Angola.

In June 1984 Thatcher received a visit from P. W. Botha, the first South African premier to come to Britain since his nation had left the Commonwealth in 1961. The leader of the opposition condemned the visit as a 'diplomatic coup' for the South African government, and Labour MEP Barbara Castle rallied European Socialists in an unsuccessful attempt to stop it. In talks at Chequers Thatcher told Botha the policy of racial separation was 'unacceptable'. She urged him to free jailed black leader Nelson Mandela; to halt the harassment of black dissidents; to stop the bombing of African National Congress (ANC) guerrilla bases in front-line states; and to comply with UN Security Council resolutions and withdraw from Namibia.

Thatcher defended Botha's visit as an encouragement to reform, but he ignored her concern over Mandela's continued detainment, and although a new constitution brought coloured people of mixed race and Indians into a tricameral assembly, 22 million blacks continued to be excluded from the representation. After the outbreak of violence in September 1984, Thatcher granted temporary sanctuary to six African anti-apartheid leaders in the British consulate in Durban.

In July 1985 Thatcher, citing the support of Helen Suzman, a South African anti-apartheid MP, reaffirmed her belief that economic sanctions against Pretoria would be immoral because they would make thousands of black workers unemployed; instead she characterised industry as the instrument that was breaking down apartheid. She also believed sanctions would disproportionately injure Britain and neighbouring African countries, and argued that political and military measures were more effective.

Thatcher's opposition to economic sanctions was challenged by visiting anti-apartheid activists, including South African bishop Desmond Tutu, whom she met in London, and Oliver Tambo, exiled leader of the outlawed ANC guerrilla movement, whose links to the Soviet bloc she viewed with suspicion, and whom she declined to see because he espoused violence and refused to condemn guerrilla attacks and mob killings of black policemen, local officials and their families.

At a Commonwealth summit in Nassau in October 1985 Thatcher agreed to impose limited sanctions and to set up a contact group to promote a dialogue with Pretoria, after she was warned by Third World leaders, including Indian prime minister Rajiv Gandhi and Malaysian prime minister Mahathir Mohamad, that her opposition threatened to break up the 49-nation organisation. In return, calls for a total embargo were abandoned, and the existing restrictions adopted by member states against South Africa were lifted. ANC president Tambo expressed disappointment at this major compromise.

Brighton bombing

On the early morning of 12 October 1984, the day before her 59th birthday, Thatcher escaped injury in the Brighton hotel bombing during the Conservative Party Conference when her hotel room was bombed by the Provisional Irish Republican Army. Five people died in the attack, including Roberta Wakeham, wife of the government's Chief Whip John Wakeham, and the Conservative MP Sir Anthony Berry. A prominent member of the Cabinet, Norman Tebbit, was injured, and his wife Margaret was left paralysed. Thatcher herself would have been injured if not for the fact that she was delayed from using the bathroom (which suffered more damage than the room she was in at the time the IRA bomb detonated). Thatcher insisted that the conference open on time the next day and made her speech as planned in defiance of the bombers, a gesture which won widespread approval across the political spectrum.

Anglo-Irish Agreement

On 15 November 1985, Thatcher signed the Hillsborough Anglo-Irish Agreement with Irish Taoiseach Garret FitzGerald, the first time a British government gave the Republic of Ireland a say (albeit advisory) in the governance of Northern Ireland. The agreement was greeted with fury by Northern Irish unionists. The Ulster Unionists and Democratic Unionists made an electoral pact and on 23 January 1986, staged an ad-hoc referendum by resigning their seats and contesting the subsequent by-elections, losing only one, to the nationalist Social Democratic and Labour Party (SDLP). However, unlike the Sunningdale Agreement of 1974, they found they could not bring the agreement down by a general strike. This was another effect of the changed balance of power in industrial relations.

Privatisation

Margaret Thatcher and Ronald Reagan at Camp David, 1986.

Thatcher's political and economic philosophy emphasised reduced state intervention, free markets, and entrepreneurialism. Since gaining power, she had experimented in selling off a small nationalised company, the National Freight Company, to its workers, with a surprisingly positive response. After the 1983 election, the Government became bolder and, starting with British Telecom, sold off most of the large utilities which had been in public ownership since the late 1940s. Many people took advantage of share offers, although many sold their shares immediately for a quick profit and therefore the proportion of shares held by individuals rather than institutions did not increase. The policy of privatisation, while anathema to many on the left, has become synonymous with Thatcherism and was also followed by Tony Blair's government. Wider share-ownership and council house sales became known as "popular capitalism" to its supporters (a term coined by John Redwood). One critic on the left described privatisation as 'the biggest electoral bribe in history'.

Cold War

In the Cold War, Thatcher supported United States President Ronald Reagan's policies of deterrence against the Soviets. This contrasted with the policy of *détente* which the West had pursued during the 1970s, and caused friction with allies who still adhered to the idea of *détente*. U.S. forces were permitted by Thatcher to station nuclear cruise missiles at British bases, arousing mass protests by the Campaign for Nuclear Disarmament. However, she later was the first Western leader to respond warmly to the rise of the future reformist Soviet leader Mikhail Gorbachev, declaring that she liked him and describing him as "a man we can do business with" after a meeting in 1984, three months before he came to power. This was a start of a move by the West back to a new *détente* with the USSR under Gorbachev's leadership, which coincided with the final erosion of Soviet power prior to its eventual collapse in 1991. Thatcher outlasted the Cold War, which ended in 1989, and those who share her views on it credit her with a part in the West's victory, by both the deterrence and *détente* postures.

The West won the Cold War 'without firing a shot', Thatcher said, because the Soviet Union would not risk confrontation with its armed forces.

Domestic criticism

In February 1985, in what was generally viewed as a significant snub from the centre of the British establishment, the University of Oxford voted to refuse Thatcher an honorary degree in protest against her cuts in funding for higher education. This award had previously been given to all prime ministers since the Second World War. Although the government's counter-claim of increased expenditure was also challenged, the decision of the Oxford dons was widely condemned as 'petty and vindictive'. The Chancellor of the university, Lord Stockton, noted that the decision represented a break with tradition, and predicted that the snub would rebound on the university.

In December 1985 Thatcher was criticised from another former Tory bastion when the Church of England report Faith in the City blamed decay of the inner cities on the government's financial stringency and called for a redistribution of wealth. However the government had already introduced special employment and training measures, and ministers dismissed the report as 'muddle-headed' and uncosted. The breach with the Church and its liberal bishops remained unhealed until William Hague called for renewed co-operation in 1998.

Soon after, Thatcher suffered her government's only defeat in the House of Commons, with the failure of the Shops Bill 1986. The bill, which would have legalised Sunday shopping, was defeated by a Christian right backbench rebellion, with 72 Conservatives voting against the government bill. As well as Thatcher's only defeat, it was the last occasion on which a government bill fell at second reading. The defeat was immediately overshadowed by the US intervention in Libya.

Bombing of Libya

In the aftermath of a series of terrorist attacks on U.S. military personnel in Europe, which were believed to have been executed at Colonel Qaddafi's command, President Reagan decided to carry out a bombing raid on Libya. Both France and Spain refused to allow U.S. aircraft to fly over their territory for the raid. Thatcher herself had earlier expressed opposition to "retaliatory strikes that are against international law" and had not followed the U.S. in an embargo of Libyan oil. However Thatcher felt that as the U.S. had given support to Britain during the Falklands War but she had opposed the U.S. invasion of Grenada and that America was a major ally against a possible Soviet attack in Western Europe, she felt obliged to allow U.S. aircraft to use bases situated in Britain. Later that year in America, President Reagan persuaded Congress to approve of an extradition treaty which closed a legal loophole by which IRA members/Volunteers escaped extradition by claiming their murders were "political". This had been previously opposed by Irish-Americans for years but was passed after Reagan used Thatcher's support in the Libyan raid as a reason to pass it.

Westland affair

Thatcher's preference for defence ties with the United States was demonstrated in the Westland affair when she acted with colleagues to allow the helicopter manufacturer Westland, a vital defence contractor, to refuse to link with the Italian firm Agusta in order for it to link with the management's preferred option, Sikorsky Aircraft Corporation of the United States. Defence Secretary Michael Heseltine, who had pushed the Agusta deal, resigned in protest after this, and remained an influential critic and potential leadership challenger. He would eventually prove instrumental in Thatcher's fall in 1990.

Local government

In April 1986 the Thatcher government, enacting a policy set out in its 1983 manifesto, abolished the Greater London Council (GLC) and six top-tier Metropolitan County Councils (MCCs): Greater Manchester, Merseyside (including Liverpool), South Yorkshire (including Sheffield), Tyne and Wear (including Newcastle and Sunderland), West Midlands (including Birmingham and Coventry), and West Yorkshire (including Leeds).

The GLC was the biggest council in Europe; under the leadership of the Labour socialist radical Ken Livingstone it had doubled its spending in three years, and Thatcher insisted on its abolition as an efficiency measure, transferring most duties to the boroughs, with veto power over major building, engineering and maintenance projects being given to the environment secretary. The government also argued that the transfer of power to local councils would increase electoral accountability.

Critics contended that 'the excesses of a few "loony left" councils helped Mrs Thatcher to launch a party-political assault', as all the eliminated councils were controlled by the Labour party, favoured higher local government taxes and public spending, and were vocal centres of opposition to her government. The GLC also warned that the break-up of the county councils would lead to the creation of 'endless joint committees and over 60 quangos'.

Several of the councils including the GLC had however rendered themselves vulnerable by committing scarce public funds to controversial causes such as Babies Against the Bomb, the Antiracist Year, and lesbian mothers seeking custody of their children; the Save the GLC campaign itself was estimated to have cost ratepayers £10 million, climaxing in a final defiant week of festivities that cost ratepayers £500,000.

Hong Kong

In 1984 Thatcher visited China and signed the Sino-British Joint Declaration with Deng Xiaoping on 19 December, which committed the People's Republic of China to award Hong Kong the status of a "Special Administrative Region". Under the terms of the One Country, Two Systems agreement, China was obliged to leave Hong Kong's economic status unchanged after the handover on 1 July 1997 for a period of fifty years – until 2047.

European rebate

At the Dublin European Council in November 1979, Thatcher argued that the United Kingdom paid far more to the European Economic Community (EEC) than it received in spending. She famously declared at the summit: "We are not asking the Community or anyone else for money. We are simply asking to have our own money back". Her arguments were successful and at the June 1984 Fontainbleau Summit, the EEC agreed on an annual rebate for the United Kingdom, amounting to 66% of the difference between Britain's EU contributions and receipts. This still remains in effect, although Tony Blair later agreed to significantly reduce the size of the rebate. It periodically causes political controversy among the members of the European Union.

Lawson boom, 1984-8

During the 1980s there was a great improvement in the United Kingdom's productivity growth relative to other advanced capitalist countries. Nigel Lawson, Chancellor of the Exchequer, identified inflation as 'the judge and jury of a government's record', but while the country also improved its OECD inflation ranking from fifteenth in 1979 to tenth in the so-called 'Lawson boom' year of 1987, when inflation had fallen to 4.2%, in the decade as a whole the country still had the second highest inflation rate of the G7 countries.

The United Kingdom's growth rate was more impressive, ranking first in the OECD-16 in 1987, a statistical achievement that the Thatcher government exploited to the full in the general election campaign of that year. However, the balance of payments record had deteriorated, faring even worse than those of non-oil-exporting countries, and there was a decline in the country's relative standing in terms of unemployment. The resulting welfare payments meant that, even though the Thatcher government in 1979 had taken the view that 'public expenditure is at the heart of Britain's present economic difficulties', it was not until the boom year of 1987 that the expenditure ratio fell below the 1979 level, and for most of the 1980s the average tax take was actually higher than in 1979.

Third government 1987–1990

1987 General election

By leading her party to victory in the 1987 general election with a 102 seat majority, riding the Lawson boom against a weak Labour opposition advocating unilateral nuclear disarmament, Margaret Thatcher became the longest continuously serving British prime minister since Lord Liverpool (1812 to 1827), and the first to win three successive elections since Lord Palmerston in 1865. Most national newspapers supported her—with the exception of *The Daily Mirror*, *The Guardian* and *The Independent*—and were rewarded with regular press briefings by her press secretary, Bernard Ingham. She was informally dubbed 'Maggie' by the tabloids, and political protesters were given to chanting the slogan 'Maggie Out!' Despite her third straight victory she remained a polarising figure, her unpopularity on the left is evident from the lyrics of several contemporary pop-music songs.

Boom to bust

The Chancellor of the Exchequer, Nigel Lawson, overreacted to a market fall with his reflationary 1988 budget, stoking inflation and precipitating a slide in the government's fortunes. By the time of Thatcher's resignation in 1990, inflation had again hit 10%, the same level she had found it in 1979.

Overall, the Thatcher government's economic record is disputed. In relative terms, it could be held there was a modest revival of British fortunes. Real gross domestic product had grown by 26.8% over 1979-89 in the United Kingdom as against 24.3% for the EC-12 average. Measured by total factor productivity, labour, and capital, British productivity growth between 1979 and 1993 compared favourably with the OECD average.

However under Thatcherite management the macro-economy was unstable, even by the standards of the Keynesian era of stop-go. The amplitude of fluctuations in gross domestic product and real gross private non-residential fixed capital formation was greater in the United Kingdom than for the OECD.

In the Thatcher years the top 10% of earners received almost 50% of the tax remissions, but there proved to be no simple trade-off between equality and efficiency. The receipts ratio did not fall below the 1979 level until 1992. The expenditure ratio rose again after Thatcher's resignation in 1990, even climbing for a time above the 1979 figure. The cause was the heavy budget charge of the recessions of 1979-81 and 1990–92 and the extra funding required to meet the higher level of unemployment.

Section 28

Though an early backer of decriminalisation of male homosexuality, Thatcher, at the 1987 Conservative party conference, issued the statement that "Children who need to be taught to respect traditional moral values are being taught that they have an inalienable right to be gay". Backbench Conservative MPs and Peers had already begun a backlash against the 'promotion' of homosexuality and, in December 1987, the controversial 'Section 28' was added as an amendment to what became the Local Government Act 1988. This legislation was repealed by Tony Blair's Labour administration between 2000 and 2003.

Welfare reforms

Welfare reforms in her third term created an adult Employment Training system that included full-time work done for the dole plus a £10 top-up, on the workfare model from the United States.

Environment

Thatcher, the former chemist, became publicly concerned with environmental issues in the late 1980s. In 1988, she made a major speech accepting the problems of global warming, ozone depletion and acid rain. In 1990, she opened the Hadley Centre for climate prediction and research. In her book *Statecraft* (2002), she described her later regret in supporting the concept of human-induced global warming, outlining the negative effects she perceived it had upon the policy-making process. "Whatever international action we agree upon to deal with environmental problems, we must enable our economies to grow and develop, because without growth you cannot generate the wealth required to pay for the protection of the environment".

European integration

At Bruges, Belgium, in 1988, Thatcher made a speech in which she outlined her opposition to proposals from the European Community for a federal structure and increasing centralisation of decision-making. Although she had supported British membership, Thatcher believed that the role of the EC should be limited to ensuring free trade and effective competition, and feared that new EC regulations would reverse the changes she was making in the UK: "We have not successfully rolled back the frontiers of the state in Britain, only to see them re-imposed at a European level, with a European super-state exercising a new dominance from Brussels". She was specifically against Economic and Monetary Union, through which a single currency would replace national currencies, and for which the EC was making preparations, now known as the euro and in force as legal tender since 2002 in twelve European countries. Britain has so far remained outside the so-called eurozone. The speech caused an outcry from other European leaders, and exposed for the first time the deep split that was emerging over European policy inside her Conservative Party.

Thatcher's popularity once again declined, in 1989, as the economy suffered from high interest rates imposed to temper a potentially unsustainable boom. She blamed her Chancellor, Nigel Lawson, who had been following an economic policy which was a preparation for monetary union; in an interview for the *Financial Times*, in November 1987, Thatcher claimed not to have been told of this and did not approve.

At a meeting before the Madrid European Community summit in June 1989, Lawson and Foreign Secretary Geoffrey Howe forced Thatcher to agree to the circumstances under which she would join the Exchange Rate Mechanism, a preparation for monetary union and the abolishment of the Pound Sterling. At the meeting, they both claimed they would resign if their demands were not met. Thatcher responded by demoting Howe and by listening more to her adviser Sir Alan Walters on economic matters. Lawson resigned that October, feeling that Thatcher had undermined him.

Leadership election, 1989

In November 1989 Thatcher was challenged for the leadership of the Conservative Party by Sir Anthony Meyer. As Meyer was a virtually unknown backbench MP, he was viewed as a "stalking horse" candidate for more prominent members of the party. Thatcher easily defeated Meyer's challenge, but there were sixty ballot papers either cast for Meyer or abstaining, a surprisingly large number for a sitting Prime Minister. Her supporters in the Party, however, viewed the results as a success, claiming that after ten years as Prime Minister and with approximately 370 Conservative MPs voting, the opposition was surprisingly small.

Release of Mandela
Thatcher continued to be the leading international advocate of a policy of contact with South Africa, and the most forthright opponent of economic sanctions against the country, which was ruled by a white minority government. Her stand had divided the Commonwealth 48-1 at three conferences since 1985, but had brought her influence in South Africa's white community. Rejecting the U.S. policy of disinvestment as a mistake, she argued a prosperous society would be more receptive to change.

In October 1988 Thatcher said she would be unlikely to visit South Africa unless black nationalist leader Nelson Mandela was released from prison, and in March 1989 she stressed the need to release him in order for multi-party talks to take place, urging that the African National Congress's promise to suspend violence should be enough to permit his release, and that the 'renunciation of violence' should not be an absolute condition for negotiations for a settlement. At the end of March 1989, Thatcher's six-day, 10,000-mile tour through southern Africa—a follow-up to her 'look and learn' exercise in Kenya and Nigeria in 1988—did not include South Africa because Mandela had not yet been released.

Thatcher met reformist South African president-in-waiting F.W. de Klerk in London in June 1989, and stressed that Mandela must be freed and reforms put in place before she would visit the country. In July 1989 she called for the release not only of Mandela, but also Walter Sisulu and Oscar Mpetha, before all-group talks could continue.

Thatcher therefore welcomed de Klerk's decision in February 1990 to release Mandela and lift the ban on the ANC, and said the change vindicated her positive policy: 'We believe in carrots as well as sticks.' However Thatcher had also set the freeing of Mandela as a condition of friendship with the white government.

Thatcher said the European Community's voluntary ban on new investment should be lifted when Mandela was released. However her call to the world to reward reforms was countered by Mandela himself, who while still in jail argued sanctions must be maintained until the end of white rule, and criticised her decision to lift a ban on new investment unilaterally. Mandela declared:

" We regard the attitude of the British Government on the question of sanctions as of primary importance ... My release from prison was the direct result of the people inside and outside South Africa. It was also the result of the immense pressure exerted on the South African Government by the international community, in particular from the people of the UK. "

However Foreign Secretary Douglas Hurd was adamant: 'We needed to make a practical response to a man, President F.W. de Klerk, who has taken his political life into his hands.' Nevertheless as a gesture of goodwill Thatcher agreed to begin aid to the ANC, which until its suspension of violence she had criticised as 'a typical terrorist organisation', her disapproval reinforced by her anti-socialism.

Mandela spoke of his respect for Thatcher, even expressing disappointment that she would not be 'the very first person I would see' on release from prison. However Thatcher's opposition to sanctions left her isolated within the Commonwealth and the European Community, and Mandela did not take up an early offer to meet her, opposing her proposed visit to his country as premature. Mandela rejected all concessions to the South African government, which he accused of seeking the easing of sanctions before it had offered 'profound and irreversible change'.

Mandela delayed meeting Thatcher until he had gathered support for sanctions from other world leaders in the course of a four-week, 14-nation tour of Europe and the United States. While Thatcher and Mandela agreed about the importance of getting rid of apartheid, their first meeting failed to resolve differences over her unilateral lifting of sanctions and his refusal to renounce armed struggle until existing conditions in South Africa changed. In their economic discussions, Mandela initially favoured nationalisation as a preferred method for redistributing wealth between blacks and whites, but with British investment in South Africa in 1989 accounting for half of the total, and with bilateral trade worth just over $3.2 billion, Thatcher successfully urged him to adopt free market solutions, arguing they would be needed to maintain the kind of growth that would sustain a liberal democratic order.

Poll tax
Thatcher sought to relieve what she considered the unfair burden of property tax on the wealthiest section of the population, and outlined a fundamental solution as her flagship policy in the Conservative manifesto for the 1987 election. Local government rates were replaced by the community charge—popularly known as the 'poll tax'—which levied a flat rate on all adult residents, with rebates for low earners, but a minimum payment of 20%.

The government defended the poll tax, firstly, on the principle of marginality, that all voters should feel the pain of local taxation, and, secondly, on the benefit principle, that burdens should be proportional to benefits received. Ministers disregarded political research which showed potential massive losses for marginal Conservative-voting households. *The Independent on Sunday* suggested:

" Tories had always expected the switch from rates, paid by 18 million people, to a com- "

munity charge, paid by 35 million, to be unpopular. But the rates were so discredited that most in the party were ready to take a chance on something new, which they were told would bring high-spending Labour councils to heel by making them responsible to the voters. If it went wrong, they could always blame the councils.

The poll tax was introduced in Scotland in 1989 and in England and Wales in 1990. This highly visible redistribution proved to be one of the most contentious policies of Thatcher's premiership. Additional problems emerged when many of the tax rates set by local councils proved to be much higher than earlier predicted. Opponents organised to resist bailiffs and disrupt court hearings of community charge debtors. One Labour MP, Terry Fields, was jailed for 60 days for refusing to pay.

An indication of the unpopularity of the policy was given by a Gallup poll in March 1990 that put Labour 18.5 points ahead. As the crisis deepened and the prime minister stood her ground, opponents claimed that up to 18 million people were refusing to pay. Enforcement measures became increasingly draconian. Unrest mounted and culminated in a number of riots. The most serious of these happened on 31 March 1990, during a protest at Trafalgar Square, London. More than 100,000 protesters attended and more than 400 people were arrested.

Tony Travers of the London School of Economics comments on the policy debacle:

" What remains to be explained is why a politician who had hitherto shown such brilliant populist sensitivity should destroy herself with a tax reform which inflicted terrible damage on millions of people who had been in the front line of the Thatcher Revolution ... Either the government failed to understand what most research and many commenta-" tors were saying, or they *did* understand it and believed that they could, as the saying went, "tough it out". A third possibility is that ministers came to understand the electoral damage ahead, but were afraid to put the case strongly enough to a Prime Minister at the helm of her "flagship".

Constitutional commentators concluded from the tax fiasco that 'the British state has become dangerously centralized, to an extent that important policy developments can now no longer be properly debated.' The unpopularity of the poll tax came to be seen as an important factor in Thatcher's downfall, by convincing many Conservative backbenchers to vote against her when she was later challenged for the leadership by Michael Heseltine.

After the prime minister's resignation, former chancellor Nigel Lawson labelled the poll tax as 'the one great blunder of the Thatcher years', and the succeeding Major government replaced it in 1993 with a council tax, a banded property tax. Former trade and industry secretary Nicholas Ridley agreed that Thatcher had suffered a massive defeat over the poll tax, but he argued that Major's repeal 'vindicated the rioters and those who had refused to pay. Lawlessness seemed to have paid off.'

Gulf War

One of Thatcher's final acts in office was to help the US , in deploying UK troops to the Middle East to drive Saddam Hussein's army out of Kuwait. Thatcher's memoirs summarise her advice to US President George H. W. Bush during a telephone conversation with the words, "this was no time to go wobbly!"

Exchange Rate Mechanism

On the Friday before the Conservative Party conference in October 1990, Thatcher ordered her new Chancellor of the Exchequer John Major to reduce interest rates by 1%. Major persuaded her that the only way to maintain monetary stability was to join the Exchange Rate Mechanism at the same time, despite not meeting the 'Madrid conditions'. The Conservative Party conference that year saw a large degree of unity; few who attended could have imagined that Thatcher had only a matter of weeks left in office.

Fall from power

Thatcher's political "assassination" was, according to witnesses such as Alan Clark, one of the most dramatic episodes in British political history. The idea of a long-serving prime minister — undefeated at the polls — being ousted by an internal party ballot might at first sight seem bizarre. However, by 1990, opposition to Thatcher's policies on local government taxation, her Government's perceived mishandling of the economy (in particular the high interest rates of 15% that eroded her support among home owners and business people), and the divisions opening in the Conservative Party over European integration made her seem increasingly politically vulnerable and her party increasingly divided. A Gallup poll in October 1990 showed that while Thatcher remained personally respected there was overwhelming opposition towards her final initiatives — 83% disapproved of the government's management of the National Health Service, 83% were against water privatisation, and 64% were against the Community Charge, while various polls suggested the party was trailing Labour by between 6 and 11 points. Moreover the prime minister's distaste for *consensus politics* and willingness to override colleagues' opinions, including that of Cabinet, emboldened the backlash against her when it did occur.

On 1 November 1990, Sir Geoffrey Howe, one of Thatcher's oldest and staunchest supporters, resigned from his position as Deputy Prime Minister in protest at Thatcher's European policy. In his resignation speech in the House of Commons two weeks later, he suggested that the time had come for "others to consider their own response to the tragic conflict of loyalties" with which he stated that he had wrestled for perhaps too long. Her former cabinet colleague Michael Heseltine subsequently challenged her for the leadership of the party, and attracted sufficient support in the first round of voting to prolong the contest to a second ballot. Though she initially stated that she intended to contest the second ballot, Thatcher decided, after consulting with her Cabinet colleagues, to withdraw from the contest. On 22 November, at just after 9.30 a.m., she announced to the Cabinet that she would not be a candidate in the second ballot. Shortly afterwards, her staff made public what was, in effect, her resignation statement:

" Having consulted widely among my colleagues, I have concluded that the unity of the Party and the prospects of victory in a General Election would be better served if I stood down to enable Cabinet colleagues to enter the ballot for the leadership. I should like to thank all those in Cabinet and outside who have given me such dedicated support. "

Neil Kinnock, Leader of the Opposition, proposed a motion of no confidence in the government, and Margaret Thatcher seized the opportunity this presented on the day of her resignation to deliver one of her most memorable performances:

" ...a single currency is about the politics of Europe, it is about a federal Europe by the back door. So I shall consider the proposal of the Honourable Member for" Bolsover (Mr. Skinner). Now where were we? *I am enjoying this.*"

She supported John Major as her successor and he duly won the leadership contest, although in the years to come her approval of Major would fall away. After her resignation a MORI poll found that 52% agreed with the proposition that "On balance she had been good for the country", while 48% disagreed thinking she had been bad. In 1991, she was given a long and unprecedented standing ovation at the party's annual conference, although she politely rejected calls from delegates for her to make a speech. She 'all but shunned' the House of Commons after losing power, and gave no clue as to her future plans, speaking only occasionally. Her continued presence was thought to be a destabilising influence on the Conservative government. She retired from the House at the 1992 election, at the age of 66 years.

Political economist Roger Middleton summed up the economic record of the Thatcher era in the following terms:

" There was no economic renaissance but a once-and-for-all catch-up exercise in labour productivity; governments have been responsible for two of the deepest depressions of the twentieth century; the experiment has generated costs which have done incalculable harm to the social fabric; and there is very little evidence that a sustain-" able new market order has been constructed since 1979. Long-standing problems of market and non-market failure remain.

Ironically, as *The Economist* acknowledged, albeit prematurely, at the close of her premiership:

" One certain beneficiary of Mrs Thatcher's radicalism has been the Labour party. She hoped to kill it, and, by 1983, it indeed seemed close to death. Instead, fear chastened it into accepting the disciplines of its new leader, Mr Neil Kinnock. True, Labour's 1983 humiliation owed much to the defection of right-wingers to form the Social Democratic party; but, in a sense, that too was her doing. Now, after years of gloomily watching her reverse the socialist 'ratchet', the Labour party has transformed itself. It has ditched unilateralism, hostility to the European Community and zeal for nationalisation. Labour as socialism is dead; as a political machine it is alive and well—and justifiably optimistic. "

Margaret Thatcher's Ministry
Source (edited): "http://en.wikipedia.org/wiki/Premiership_of_Margaret_Thatcher"

Public Bodies (Admission to Meetings) Act 1960

The **Public Bodies (Admission to Meetings) Act** was an act of the Parliament of the United Kingdom in 1960 which allowed members of the public and press to attend meetings of certain public bodies. The Act is notable for being proposed by a private member's bill drawn up by Margaret Thatcher, and also for being introduced as a maiden speech, a unique feat for successful legislation, on 5 February 1960 Her maiden speech was delivered without notes, and was lauded as the best maiden speech amongst the 1959 new intake.

It was introduced primarily to prevent circumvention of rules prohibiting councils from excluding the press by calling a Committee of the Whole: a tactic that had been used by Labour-controlled councils during an industrial dispute in the printing industry in 1958. A similar bill had been introduced years earlier by Lionel Heald, who helped guide Thatcher through the legislative process.

Source (edited): "http://en.wikipedia.org/wiki/Public_Bodies_(Admission_to_Meetings)_Act_1960"

Sanctuary (Iron Maiden song)

"**Sanctuary**" is the second single released by the British heavy metal band Iron Maiden. The single was released on 23 May 1980. The song was included in the US release of their debut album *Iron Maiden* but it was not included in the UK/European release. However, when the album was re-released in 1998 the song was added to the UK release.

The cover art shows the band's mascot, Eddie having just murdered former Prime Minister, Margaret Thatcher. This image, though intended as a lighthearted play on her nickname as the "Iron Lady", managed to cause a minor stir in local newspapers (though this was nothing compared with the reaction to one of their future albums). On most copies of the original single, Thatcher's eyes were covered by a black box because the image was considered offensive. Copies without this box are extremely rare, however are not to be confused with The First Ten Years 12" rerelease, which no longer features the black box. When Derek Riggs was asked about the artwork during "The First Ten Years" documentary, he said that he'd originally drawn the cover featuring Eddie murdering another woman, inspired by the line in the song "I never killed a woman before but I know how it feels", but when he took the art to the band they asked him to change it to include Margaret Thatcher. Of the incident, he said, "they wanted me to make it look like Margaret Thatcher, because she was called the Iron Maiden, but I didn't even have a photograph of the woman!" He wound up having to contact Margaret Thatcher's Public Relations people, who then sent him a photo of her.

"Sanctuary" was originally released in both 7" and 12" 45rpm vinyl formats. The 12" included "Prowler" as an extra song on the A-side. The b-side includes a live version of the song "Drifter" and a live version of Montrose's "I've Got the Fire", from their 1974 album *Paper Money*. "Drifter" includes the usual crowd interaction part where the audience is invited to follow the lead singer as he chants "Yo Yo Yo", parodying The Police song "Walking on the Moon" Both of the songs were recorded live at the Marquee Club in London on 3 April 1980.

On "Sanctuary", the first guitar solo is played by Dennis Stratton followed by a guitar solo by Dave Murray. On both the live versions of "Drifter" and "I've Got the Fire", the first guitar solo is played by Murray while the second is played by Stratton.

On live performances of the song, the band would always slip in the opening guitar riff of Queen's "Keep Yourself Alive" on the final portion of the instrumental section. During more modern performances, guitarist Janick Gers will normally create a large amount of guitar feedback and noise on his guitar before playing the riff. In live versions, singer Bruce Dickinson will sing a long "Yeah!" after the first verse. It is one of Iron Maiden's most frequently played songs, being played in almost every tour up to the present day.

An alternate recording of the song was featured on the NWOBHM Metal for Muthas compilation.

Track listing
- "Sanctuary" (Harris, Di'Anno, Murray) - 3:14
- "Prowler (Harris) -3:52
- "Drifter (Live at the Marquee, London 1980)" (Harris) - 6:03
- "I've Got the Fire (Live at the Marquee, London 1980)" (Ronnie Montrose; Montrose cover) - 3:14

Personnel
- Paul Di'Anno - vocals
- Dave Murray - guitar
- Dennis Stratton - guitar, backing vocals
- Steve Harris - bass guitar, backing vocals
- Clive Burr - drums

Source (edited): "http://en.wikipedia.org/wiki/Sanctuary_(Iron_Maiden_song)"

Shops Bill 1986

The **Shops Bill 1986** was a parliamentary bill in the United Kingdom that would have ended government regulation of Sunday shopping in England and Wales. Introduced by the government of Margaret Thatcher, it was defeated in the House of Commons at its second reading: the last time that a government bill had fallen at that stage.

The Shops Act 1950 regulated Sunday shopping hours, making it illegal for shops to sell most products on Sunday. The Auld Committee, chaired by Robin Auld, found that the regime established by the 1950 act was unworkable, with arbitrary exemptions and widespread breaches by large retailers. The consequent Auld Report recommended that the Shops Act be repealed, which the government accepted and adopted into its legislative programme.

Thatcher had anticipated that Labour would oppose the bill, spurred by trade unions fears that shop-workers would be forced to work on Sundays. However, she did not anticipate the backlash from the Christian right. 72 Conservative backbenchers defied a three line whip, voting against the bill at second reading – just after midnight on the morning of 15 April 1986 – and it was defeated by 14 votes. This represented Thatcher's only defeat in the House of Commons.

Sunday trading was ultimately relaxed by the Sunday Trading Act 1994: the 27th attempt to do so.

Source (edited): "http://en.wikipedia.org/wiki/Shops_Bill_1986"

Statecraft: Strategies for a Changing World

Statecraft: Strategies for a Changing World is a book on politics and international relations written by Margaret Thatcher in 2003 and was published by Harper Perennial.

Synopsis
Looking at the lessons learnt during the Cold War Lady Thatcher writes of the United States being the only remaining superpower, and the responsibilities which come with that burden.

She also writes about the dangers inherent in the Balkans given the instability of the region and the rise of Islamic Extremism.

Reception
Bill Emmott writing in the Los Angeles Times said, "Europeans, Asians, Latin Americans (except Pinochet) and Africans simply don't have a chance in Thatcher's eyes. They do not trace back their political and legal values to the Magna Carta. They are all, in her eyes, collectivists rather than freedom-loving individuals. It is all the more surprising therefore that having supported British membership of the European Union during the 1970s and having helped to deepen that market during her time as prime minister, she now thinks Britain ought to leave that ghastly grouping, run as it is by bureaucrats and foreigners. To be critical of European countries and of the European institutions is fine: There is plenty to criticize and to change. But in this book Thatcher goes beyond that, arguing in essence that Europe is always to be distrusted because it is full of Europeans and in her lifetime Europeans have always caused trouble."

Francis Maude writing for the New Statesman said, "Thatcher's latest and, she says, last book is not really what it says. Its title suggests a manual for practitioners of statecraft, a sort of Macchiavelli's The Prince for our times. Such practitioners will find Statecraft well worth reading, as will all those with an interest in international affairs, because this is an account of Thatcher's views about the world, its recent histories and what should be done. It is broad in scope, detailed in analysis and, as you would expect, forthright in prescription. And prescription is in plentiful supply".

Michael Collins has written in Contemporary Review, "Statecraft is aimed as much at decision-makers in the US as at a domestic readership. In fact fewer than a fifth of the book's magisterial and incisive survey of current world affairs is concerned with the European Union. Most of it is composed of observations derived from meetings with world leaders and briefings from well-placed sources. Lady Thatcher takes a typically no-nonsense approach to the realities of power politics and warns that battlefield nuclear weapons will be used in the foreseeable future. Yet 'since the end of the Cold War' she argues, 'the West has let down its guard'. Two powers came out big winners at the end of the Cold War: the United States and China".

Source (edited): "http://en.wikipedia.org/wiki/Statecraft:_Strategies_for_a_Changing_World"

Thatcher's England

Thatcher's England is a derogatory term for England during the 1980s, all of which fell under the tenure of Margaret Thatcher as Prime Minister. The term is most often used to portray an oppressive, almost-Orwellian status quo that punk and other youth cultures were rebellious against; the preface to Alan Moore's *V for Vendetta* mentions England under an oppressive government called Norsefire in an alternate-future-now-past 1997/8, this happens after a nuclear war in 1988, which England manages to escape as it has been disarmed by Michael Foot after he won the 1983 General Election (The whole comic is based on the question: "What would happen if Thatcher had lost the 1983 Election?) as a major influence on its dystopian setting, retrospectives of 80s punk rock bands often cite the influence of "Thatcher's England" on the bands' sound, and in the 1980s BBC comedy series *The Young Ones*, the character Rik repeatedly complains about how things are in "Thatcher's England", citing it as the source of most of his troubles (whether relevant or not).

Source (edited): "http://en.wikipedia.org/wiki/Thatcher%27s_England"

Thatcher ministry

Margaret Thatcher, Prime Minister (1979 - 1990)

Margaret Thatcher was the Prime Minister of the United Kingdom between 4 May 1979 and 28 November 1990, during which time she led a Conservative government. She was the first woman to hold that office. During her premiership, Thatcher moved to modernise the British economy and promote free markets and entrepreneurialism.

Cabinets listed chronologically

These are the cabinets under Prime Minister Margaret Thatcher (from May 1979 to November 1990).

Cabinet May 1979–September 1981

- Margaret Thatcher: Prime Minister
- William Whitelaw: Deputy Prime Minister and Home Secretary
- Sir Geoffrey Howe: Chancellor of the Exchequer
- John Biffen: Chief Secretary to the Treasury
- Lord Soames: Lord President of the Council
- Lord Hailsham of St Marylebone: Lord Chancellor
- Sir Ian Gilmour: Lord Privy Seal
- Lord Carrington: Foreign Secretary
- Peter Walker: Minister of Agriculture, Fisheries and Food
- Norman St John-Stevas: Minister for the Arts and Chancellor of the Duchy of Lancaster
- Francis Pym: Secretary for Defence
- Mark Carlisle: Secretary of State for Education and Science
- James Prior: Secretary of State for Employment
- David Howell: Secretary of State for Energy
- Michael Heseltine: Secretary of State for the Environment
- Patrick Jenkin: Secretary of State for Health and Social Security
- Keith Joseph: Secretary of State for Industry
- Humphrey Atkins: Secretary of State for Northern Ireland
- Angus Maude: Paymaster-General
- George Younger: Secretary of State for Scotland
- John Nott: Secretary of State for Trade and President of the Board of Trade
- Nicholas Edwards: Secretary of State for Wales
- Michael Jopling: Chief Whip
- Michael Havers: Attorney General

Changes

- January 1981: Francis Pym succeeds Norman St John-Stevas as Chancellor of the Duchy of Lancaster. Pym succeeds Angus Maude as Paymaster-General. John Nott succeeds Pym as Secretary of State for Defence. John Biffen succeeds Nott as Secretary of State for Trade and President of the Board of Trade. Leon Brittan succeeds John Biffen as Chief Secretary to the Treasury. St John-Stevas resigns as Minister for the Arts. His successor is not in the cabinet. The post of Secretary of State for Transport is brought into the cabinet and Norman Fowler is given the post.

Cabinet September 1981–June 1983

September 1981: A substantial reshuffle took place:

- Margaret Thatcher: Prime Minister
- William Whitelaw: Deputy Prime Minister and Secretary of State for the Home Department
- Geoffrey Howe: Chancellor of the Exchequer
- Leon Brittan: Chief Secretary to the Treasury
- Francis Pym: Lord President of the Council
- Lord Hailsham of St Marylebone: Lord Chancellor
- Humphrey Atkins: Lord Privy Seal
- Lord Carrington: Secretary of State for Foreign and Commonwealth Affairs
- Peter Walker: Minister of Agriculture, Fisheries and Food
- John Nott: Secretary of State for Defence
- Sir Keith Joseph: Secretary of State for Education and Science
- Norman Tebbit: Secretary of State for Employment
- Nigel Lawson: Secretary of State for Energy
- Michael Heseltine: Secretary of State for the Environment
- Norman Fowler: Secretary of State for Health and Social Security
- Patrick Jenkin: Secretary of State for Industry
- Baroness Young: Chancellor of the Duchy of Lancaster
- James Prior: Secretary of State for Northern Ireland
- Cecil Parkinson: Paymaster-General
- George Younger: Secretary of State for Scotland
- John Biffen: Secretary of State for Trade and President of the Board of Trade
- David Howell: Secretary of State for Transport
- Nicholas Edwards: Secretary of State for Wales

Changes

- April 1982: Francis Pym succeeds

Lord Carrington as Foreign Secretary. John Biffen succeeds Pym as Lord President of the Council. Baroness Young succeeds Humphrey Atkins as Lord Privy Seal. Cecil Parkinson succeeds Baroness Young as Chancellor of the Duchy of Lancaster. Lord Cockfield succeeds John Biffen as Secretary of State for Trade.
- January 1983: Michael Heseltine succeeds John Nott as Secretary of State for Defence. Tom King succeeds Heseltine as Secretary of State for the Environment.

Cabinet June 1983–June 1987

- Margaret Thatcher - Prime Minister
- Lord Whitelaw: Deputy Prime Minister and Lord President of the Council
- Lord Hailsham of St Marylebone: Lord Chancellor
- John Biffen: Lord Privy Seal
- Nigel Lawson: Chancellor of the Exchequer
- Peter Rees: Chief Secretary to the Treasury
- Sir Geoffrey Howe: Secretary of State for Foreign and Commonwealth Affairs
- Leon Brittan: Secretary of State for the Home Department
- Michael Jopling: Minister of Agriculture, Fisheries and Food
- Michael Heseltine: Secretary of State for Defence
- Sir Keith Joseph: Secretary of State for Education and Science
- Norman Tebbit: Secretary of State for Employment
- Peter Walker: Secretary of State for Energy
- Patrick Jenkin: Secretary of State for the Environment
- Norman Fowler: Secretary of State for Health
- Lord Cockfield: Chancellor of the Duchy of Lancaster
- James Prior: Secretary of State for Northern Ireland
- George Younger: Secretary of State for Scotland
- Cecil Parkinson: Secretary of State for Trade and Industry
- Tom King: Secretary of State for Transport
- Nicholas Edwards: Secretary of State for Wales
- John Wakeham: Chief Whip

Changes

- October 1983: Tom King succeeds Norman Tebbit as Secretary of State for Employment. Norman Tebbit succeeds Cecil Parkinson as Secretary of State for Trade and Industry. Nicholas Ridley succeeds Tom King as Secretary of State for Transport.
- September 1984: Lord Gowrie succeeds Lord Cockfield as Chancellor of the Duchy of Lancaster. Douglas Hurd succeeds James Prior as Secretary of State for Northern Ireland. Lord Young of Graffham enters the cabinet as Minister without Portfolio.
- September 1985: Lord Young of Graffham succeeds Tom King as Secretary of State for Employment. Kenneth Baker succeeds Patrick Jenkin as Secretary of State for the Environment. Norman Tebbit succeeds Lord Gowrie as Chancellor of the Duchy of Lancaster. Tom King succeeds Douglas Hurd as Secretary of State for Northern Ireland. Kenneth Clarke enters the cabinet as Paymaster-General. Leon Brittan succeeds Norman Tebbit as Secretary of State for Trade and Industry. John MacGregor succeeds Peter Rees as Chief Secretary to the Treasury. Douglas Hurd succeeds Leon Brittan as Home Secretary.
- Early January 1986: Malcolm Rifkind succeeds George Younger as Secretary of State for Scotland. Younger succeeds Michael Heseltine as Secretary of State for Defence.
- Late January 1986: Paul Channon succeeds Leon Brittan as Secretary of State for Trade and Industry.
- May 1986: Nicholas Ridley succeeds Kenneth Baker as Secretary of State for the Environment. John Moore succeeds Nicholas Ridley as Secretary of State for Transport. Kenneth Baker succeeds Keith Joseph as Secretary of State for Education and Science.

Cabinet June 1987–July 1989

- Margaret Thatcher - Prime Minister
- Lord Whitelaw: Deputy Prime Minister and Lord President of the Council
- Lord Havers: Lord Chancellor
- John Wakeham: Lord Privy Seal
- Nigel Lawson: Chancellor of the Exchequer
- John Major: Chief Secretary to the Treasury
- Geoffery Howe: Secretary of State for Foreign and Commonwealth Affairs
- Douglas Hurd: Secretary of State for the Home Department
- John MacGregor: Minister of Agriculture, Fisheries and Food
- George Younger: Secretary of State for Defence
- Kenneth Baker: Secretary of State for Education and Science
- Norman Fowler: Secretary of State for Employment
- Cecil Parkinson: Secretary of State for Energy
- Nicholas Ridley: Secretary of State for the Environment
- John Moore: Secretary of State for Health
- Kenneth Clarke: Chancellor of the Duchy of Lancaster
- Tom King: Secretary of State for Northern Ireland
- Malcolm Rifkind: Secretary of State for Scotland
- Lord Young of Graffham: Secretary of State for Trade and Industry
- Paul Channon: Secretary of State for Transport
- Peter Walker: Secretary of State for Wales
- David Waddington: Chief Whip
- Sir Patrick Mayhew: Attorney General

Changes

- October 1987: Lord Mackay of Clashfern succeeds Lord Havers as Lord Chancellor.
- January 1988: Lord Whitelaw retires and is succeeded by John Wakeham as Lord President; no new Deputy

Prime Minister is appointed until July 1989. Lord Belstead succeeds Wakeham as Lord Privy Seal.
- July 1988: Department of Health and Social Security broken up into component parts. John Moore continues on as Secretary of State for Social Security. Kenneth Clarke becomes Secretary of State for Health. Tony Newton succeeds Clarke as Chancellor of the Duchy of Lancaster.

Cabinet July 1989–November 1990

July 1989: Reshuffle:
- Margaret Thatcher - Prime Minister
- Sir Geoffrey Howe: Deputy Prime Minister and Lord President of the Council
- Lord Mackay of Clashfern: Lord Chancellor
- Lord Belstead: Lord Privy Seal
- Nigel Lawson: Chancellor of the Exchequer
- Norman Lamont: Chief Secretary to the Treasury
- John Major: Secretary of State for Foreign and Commonwealth Affairs
- Douglas Hurd: Secretary of State for the Home Department
- John Gummer: Minister of Agriculture, Fisheries and Food
- Tom King: Secretary of State for Defence
- John MacGregor: Secretary of State for Education and Science
- Norman Fowler: Secretary of State for Employment
- John Wakeham: Secretary of State for Energy
- Chris Patten: Secretary of State for the Environment
- Kenneth Clarke: Secretary of State for Health
- Kenneth Baker: Chancellor of the Duchy of Lancaster
- Peter Brooke: Secretary of State for Northern Ireland
- Malcolm Rifkind: Secretary of State for Scotland
- Tony Newton: Secretary of State for Social Security
- Nicholas Ridley: Secretary of State for Trade and Industry
- Cecil Parkinson: Secretary of State for Transport
- Peter Walker: Secretary of State for Wales

Changes
- October 1989: John Major succeeds Nigel Lawson as Chancellor of the Exchequer. Douglas Hurd succeeds John Major as Secretary of State for Foreign and Commonwealth Affairs. David Waddington succeeds Douglas Hurd as Secretary of State for the Home Department. Tim Renton succeeds David Waddington as Chief Whip.
- January 1990: Norman Fowler resigns as Secretary of State for Employment and is succeeded by Michael Howard.
- May 1990: Peter Walker finally resigns as Secretary of State for Wales having announced his intentions in March. David Hunt succeeds him.
- July 1990: Nicholas Ridley resigns as Secretary of State for Trade & Industry. Peter Lilley succeeds him.
- November 1990: At the start of the month Geoffrey Howe resigns and the title of Deputy Prime Minister was not reallocated. John MacGregor succeeds him as Lord President of the Council and is in turn succeeded by Kenneth Clarke as Secretary of State for Education and Science who is succeeded by William Waldegrave as Secretary of State for Health.

Source (edited): "http://en.wikipedia.org/wiki/Thatcher_ministry"

Thatcherism

Thatcherism describes the conviction politics, economic and social policy, and political style of the British Conservative politician Margaret Thatcher, who was leader of her party from 1975 to 1990. It has also been used by some to describe the ideology and wider political culture of the British government while Thatcher was Prime Minister between May 1979 and November 1990, and beyond into the governments of John Major, Tony Blair, Gordon Brown and David Cameron.

Overview

Margaret Thatcher

Thatcherism claims to promote low inflation, the small state and free markets through tight control of the money supply, privatisation and constraints on the labour movement. It is often compared with Reaganomics in the United States, Rogernomics in New Zealand and Economic Rationalism in Australia as a key part of the worldwide neoliberal movement. Nigel Lawson, Thatcher's Chancellor of the Exchequer from 1983 to 1989, listed the Thatcherite ideals as: Free markets, financial discipline, firm control over public expenditure, tax cuts, nationalism, 'Victorian values' (of the Samuel Smiles self-help variety), privatisation and a dash of populism.

Thatcherism is thus often compared to classical liberalism. Milton Friedman claimed that "the thing that people do not recognise is that Margaret Thatcher is not in terms of belief a Tory. She is a nineteenth-century Liberal." Thatcher herself stated in 1983: "I would not mind betting that if Mr Gladstone were alive today he would apply to join the Conservative Party". In the 1996 Keith Joseph memorial lecture Mrs. Thatcher argued that "The kind of Conservatism which he and I...favoured would be best described as 'liberal', in the old-fashioned sense. And I mean the liberalism of Mr. Gladstone, not of the latter day collectivists". Thatcher once told Friedrich Hayek: "I know you want me to become a Whig; no, I am a Tory". Hayek believed "she has felt this very clearly".

But the relationship between Thatcherism and liberalism is complicated. Thatcher's former Defence Secretary John Nott claimed that "it is a complete misreading of her beliefs to depict her as a nineteenth-century Liberal". As Ellen Meiksins Wood has argued, Thatcherite capitalism was compatible with old-fashioned conservative political institutions. As Prime Minister, Thatcher challenged, not ancient bodies like the monarchy and the House of Lords, but some of the most recent additions to British politics: the trade unions. Indeed, many leading Thatcherites, including Thatcher herself, went on to join the House of Lords: an honour which Gladstone, for instance, had declined.

Thinkers closely associated with Thatcherism include Keith Joseph, Enoch Powell, Friedrich Hayek and Milton Friedman. In an interview with Simon Heffer in 1996 Thatcher stated that the two greatest influences on her as Conservative leader had been Joseph and Powell, "both of them very great men".

Thatcherism before Thatcher

A number of commentators have traced the origins of Thatcherism in post-war British politics. The late historian Ewen Green identified a strain of resentment to the inflation, taxation and the limited constraints on the labour movement associated with the so-called Buttskellite consensus in the decades before Thatcher herself came to prominence. Although the Conservative leadership accommodated itself to the Attlee government's post-war reforms, there was continuous right-wing opposition in the lower ranks of the party, in right-wing pressure groups like the Middle Class Alliance and the People's League for the Defence of Freedom, and later in think tanks like the Centre for Policy Studies. For example, in 1945 the Conservative Party Chairman Ralph Assheton had wanted 12,000 abridged copies of *The Road to Serfdom* (a book by the anti-socialist economist Friedrich von Hayek later closely associated with Thatcherism), taking up one-and-a-half tons of the party's paper ration, distributed as election propaganda.

Libertarianism

Thatcherism is often described as a libertarian ideology. Thatcher saw herself as creating a libertarian movement, rejecting traditional Toryism. Thatcherism is associated with libertarianism within the Conservative Party, albeit one of libertarian ends achieved by using strong and sometimes authoritarian leadership. Andrew Marr has called libertarianism the 'dominant, if unofficial, characteristic of Thatcherism'. However, whereas some of her heirs, notably Michael Portillo and Alan Duncan, embraced this libertarianism, others in the Thatcherite movement, such as John Redwood, became more populist.

However, some commentators have argued that Thatcherism should not be considered properly libertarian. Noting the tendency towards strong central government in matters concerning the trade unions and local authorities, Andrew Gamble summarised Thatcherism as 'the free economy and the strong state'. Simon Jenkins accused the Thatcher government of carrying out a 'nationalisation' of Britain.

Thatcherite economics

Thatcherism is associated with the economic theory of monetarism. In contrast to previous government policy, monetarism placed a priority on controlling inflation over controlling unemployment. According to monetarist theory, inflation is the result of there being too much money in the economy. Thus the government should control the money supply to control inflation. However, by 1979 it was not only the Thatcherites who were arguing for stricter control of inflation. The Labour Chancellor Denis Healey had already adopted some monetarist policies, such as reducing public spending and selling off the government's shares in BP.

Moreover, it has been argued that the

Thatcherites themselves were not strictly monetarist in practice. A common theme centres on the Medium Term Financial Strategy. The Strategy, issued in the 1980 Budget, consisted of targets for reducing the growth of the money supply in the following years. After overshooting many of these targets, the Thatcher government revised the targets upwards in 1982. Analysts have interpreted this as an admission of defeat in the battle to control the money supply. The economist C. F. Pratten claimed:

Since 1984, behind a veil of rhetoric, the government has lost any faith it had in technical monetarism. The money supply, as measured by £M3, has been allowed to grow erratically, while calculation of the PSBR is held down by the ruse of subtracting the proceeds of privatisation as well as taxes from government expenditure. The principles of monetarism have been abandoned.

Thatcherism is also associated with supply-side economics. Whereas Keynesian economics holds that the government should stimulate economic growth by increasing demand through increased credit and public spending, supply-side economists argue that the government should instead intervene only to create a free market by lowering taxes, privatizing state industries and increasing restraints on trade unionism.

Trade union legislation

Reduction in the power of the trades unions was made gradually, unlike the approach of the Heath Government, and the greatest single confrontation with the unions was the NUM strike of 1984 to 1985, in which the union eventually had to concede.

Thatcherite morality

Thatcherism is associated with a conservative stance on morality. The sociologist and founder of the New Left Review, Stuart Hall, for example, argued that Thatcherism should be viewed as an ideological project promoting "authoritarian populism," since it is known its reverence to "Victorian values." David Marquand expressed the "authoritarian populist" sentiment in 1970s Britain that Thatcherism supposedly exploited: "Go back, you flower people, back where you came from, wash your hair, get dressed properly, get to work on time and stop all this whingeing and moaning." Norman Tebbit, a close ally of Thatcher, laid out in a 1985 lecture what he thought to be the permissive society that conservatives should oppose: Bad art was as good as good art. Grammar and spelling were no longer important. To be clean was no better than to be filthy. Good manners were no better than bad. Family life was derided as a outdated bourgeois concept. Criminals deserved as much sympathy as their victims. Many homes and classrooms became disorderly - if there was neither right nor wrong there could be no bases for punishment or reward. Violence and soft pornography became accepted in the media. Thus was sown the wind; and we are now reaping the whirlwind.

Examples of this conservative morality in practice include the video nasties scare, where, in reaction to a moral panic over the availability of a number of provocatively named horror films on video cassette, Thatcher introduced state regulation of the British video market for the first time.

Thatcher is generally characterised as having being opposed to gay rights, primarily due to the introduction of Section 28, which forbade schools, libraries and other public bodies from promoting homosexuality. Furthermore, at the 1987 Conservative Conference, she said "Children… are being taught that they have an inalienable right to be gay".

Sermon on the Mound

In May 1988 Thatcher gave an address to the General Assembly of the Church of Scotland. In the address, Thatcher offered a theological justification for her ideas on capitalism and the market economy. She claimed "Christianity is about spiritual redemption, not social reform" and she quoted St Paul by saying "If a man will not work he shall not eat". 'Choice' played a significant part in Thatcherite reforms and Thatcher claimed choice was also Christian by stating that Christ chose to lay down his life and that all individuals have the God-given right to choose between good and evil.

Europe

Towards the end of the 1980s Margaret Thatcher, and so Thatcherism, became increasingly vocal in its opposition to allowing the European Union to supersede British sovereignty. In her famous 1988 Bruges speech, Thatcher declared that "We have not successfully rolled back the frontiers of the state in Britain, only to see them reimposed at a European level, with a European superstate exercising a new dominance from Brussels".

While euro-scepticism has for many become a characteristic of "Thatcherism", Margaret Thatcher was far from consistent on the issue, only becoming truly Eurosceptic in the last years of her time as Prime Minister. Thatcher supported Britain's entry into the European Economic Community in 1973, campaigned for a yes vote in the 1975 referendum and signed the Single European Act in 1986.

Thatcherism as a form of government

Another important aspect of Thatcherism is the style of governance. Britain in the 1970s was often referred to as "ungovernable". Mrs Thatcher attempted to redress this by centralising a great deal of power to herself, as the Prime Minister, often bypassing traditional cabinet structures (such as cabinet committees). This personal approach also became identified with a certain toughness at times such as the Falklands War, the IRA bomb at the Conservative conference and the Miner's Strike.

Sir Charles Powell, the Foreign Affairs Private Secretary to the Prime Minister (1984-91, 96) described her style thus, "I've always thought there was something Leninist about Mrs. Thatcher which came through in the style of government — the absolute determination, the belief that there's a vanguard which is right and if you keep that small, tightly knit team together, they will drive things through … there's no doubt that in the 1980s, No. 10 could beat the bushes of Whitehall pretty violently. They could go out and really confront people, lay down the law, bully a bit".

Dispute over the term

It is often claimed that the word "Thatcherism" was coined by cultural theorist Stuart Hall in a 1979 Marxism Today article, although the term had in fact been widely used before then. However, not all social critics have accepted the term as valid, with the High Tory journalist T. E. Utley believing that "There is no such thing as Thatcherism." Utley contended that the term was a creation of Mrs. Thatcher's enemies who wished to damage her by claiming that she had an inflexible devotion to a certain set of principles and also by some of her friends who, "for cultural and sometimes ethnic reasons" had little sympathy with what he described as the "English political tradition." Thatcher was not an ideologue, Utley further argued, but a pragmatic politician; giving examples of her refusal to radically reform the welfare state and the need to avoid a miners' strike in 1981 at a time when the Government was not ready to handle it.

On another hand some claim that Thatcherism was moved actually by pure ideology and that her policies marked a turning point in economic policies which were dictated more by reasons of political power and interests than actually by economic reasons:

Rather than by any specific logic of capitalism, the reversal was brought about by voluntary reductions in social expenditures, higher taxes on low incomes and the lowering of taxes on higher incomes. This is the reason why in Great Britain in the mid 1980s the members of the top decile possessed more than a half of all the wealth (Giddens 1993, 233). To justify this by means of economic "objectivities" would be an ideology. What is at play here are interests and power.

The Conservative historian of Peterhouse, Maurice Cowling, also questioned the uniqueness of "Thatcherism". Cowling claimed that Mrs. Thatcher used "radical variations on that patriotic conjunction of freedom, authority, inequality, individualism and average decency and respectability, which had been the Conservative Party's theme since at least 1886." Cowling further contended that the "Conservative Party under Mrs. Thatcher has used a radical rhetoric to give intellectual respectability to what the Conservative Party has always wanted."

Criticism

Critics of Thatcherism claim that its successes were obtained only at the expense of great social costs to the British population. Industrial production fell sharply during Thatcher's government, which critics believe increased unemployment — which tripled by 1984 (though receded to one and a half the level she inherited by 1990). When she resigned in 1990, 28% of the children in Great Britain were considered to be below the poverty line, a number that kept rising to reach a peak of 30% in 1994 during the Conservative government of John Major, who succeeded Thatcher.

While credited with reviving Britain's economy, Mrs. Thatcher also was blamed for spurring a doubling in the poverty rate. Britain's childhood-poverty rate in 1997 was the highest in Europe.

During her government Britain's Gini coefficient reflected this growing inequality, going from 0.25 in 1979 to 0.34 in 1990.

Thatcher's legacy

The extent to which one can say 'Thatcherism' has a continuing influence on British political and economic life is unclear. In 2001, Peter Mandelson, a Member of Parliament belonging to the British Labour Party closely associated with Tony Blair, famously declared that "we are all Thatcherites now."

In reference to contemporary British political culture, it could be said that a "post-Thatcherite consensus" exists, especially in regards to economic policy. In the 1980s, the now defunct Social Democratic Party adhered to a "tough and tender" approach in which Thatcherite reforms were coupled with extra welfare provision. Neil Kinnock, leader of the Labour Party from 1983-1992, initiated Labour's rightward shift across the political spectrum by largely concurring with the economic policies of the Thatcher governments. The New Labour governments of Tony Blair and Gordon Brown were described as "neo-Thatcherite" by some, since many of their economic policies mimicked those of Thatcher.

Most of the major British political parties today accept the anti-trade union legislation, privatisations and general free market approach to government that Thatcher's governments installed. No major political party in the UK, at present, is committed to reversing the Thatcher government's reforms of the economy. Such a convergence of policy is one reason that the British electorate perceive few apparent differences in policy between the major political parties.

Moreover, the UK's comparative macroeconomic performance has improved since the implementation of Thatcherite economic policies. Since Thatcher resigned as British Prime Minister in 1990, UK economic growth was on average higher than the other large EU economies (i.e. Germany, France and Italy). Additionally, since the beginning of the 2000s, the UK has also possessed lower unemployment, by comparison with the other big EU economies. Such an enhancement in relative macroeconomic performance is perhaps another reason for the apparent "Blatcherite" economic consensus, which has been present in modern UK politics for a number of years.

On the occasion of the 25th anniversary of Thatcher's inauguration, BBC conducted a survey of opinions which opened with the following comments:

To her supporters, she was a revolutionary figure who transformed Britain's stagnant economy, tamed the unions and re-established the country as a world power.

Together with US presidents Reagan and Bush, she helped bring about the end of the Cold War.

But her 11-year premiership was also marked by social unrest, industrial strife and high unemployment.

Her critics claim British society is still feeling the effect of her divisive economic policies and the culture of greed and selfishness they allegedly promoted.

Source (edited): "http://en.wikipedia.org/wiki/Thatcherism"

There Is No Alternative: Why Margaret Thatcher Matters

There Is No Alternative: Why Margaret Thatcher Matters is a 2008 biographical account of the premiership of Margaret Thatcher written by American author Claire Berlinski.

The title is a reference to Margaret Thatcher's fondness for the slogan "There is no alternative" which she used to describe her belief that despite capitalism's problems, "there is no alternative" to it as an economic system, and that neoliberalism must push back against socialism. The phrase became something of a rallying cry of arguments in favor of free markets, free trade, and capitalist globalization, with Thatcher and her followers believing that it is the only way which modern societies can advance themselves.

The primary focus of the biography is a favorable account of the Thatcher years, arguing that much like Thatcher's ideology, there was no alternative after the malaise of the 1970s, but to embrace a leader like Thatcher. Berlinski argues that much of how the world is currently organized today is as a result of her, and because of this she matters to modern society even today.

Overview

There Is No Alternative is an attempt by the author to explore the rise and success of Prime Minister Margaret Thatcher who Berlinski argues was an important and remarkable leader. It credits Thatcher with the transformation of British society from an empire eternally in decline with a weak economy and an irrelevant political culture to a modern, wealthy, influential nation. The comeback of the United Kingdom mirrors that of Thatchers own rise from lower-middle class beginnings. Berlinski credits her with being the catalyst for the deconstruction of the post-war socialistic policies of Europe, and the rise of the global free-market revolution.

Berlinski uses archival research, author accounts as a person living through the Thatcher years in the United Kingdom, and a number of interviews to examine Thatcher's rise to power, what drove her crusade against socialism, the importance of her victories and the costs to the country her transformation caused. Berlinski argues that Thatcher was able to achieve power and influence that no woman before her was able to do, and that she used her femininity for political purposes to help advance her push back against socialism.

The author claims to be "on her side", yet also takes a somewhat frank and cold look at the negative aspects of Thatcher's reign. The text outlines what Berlinski describes as the failures of monetarism and the bitter social issues her policies helped create in Britain. Yet she argues that despite her failures, her significance and impact on British society can not be refuted.

Berlinski has said that her goal in writing this biography was to inform, but also entertain the reader. She attempts to give the text a dramatic treatment which will recreate Thatcher's personality and the environment she was surrounded with. She argues that it is not an academic work, but rather a work of popular non-fiction.

Critical reception

In *The New York Times* Stephen Pollard called it "an immensely frustrating book, the whole being less than the sum of its rather incompatible parts."

Theodore Dalrymple took a favorable view of the biography, writing in the *Globe and Mail*: "Without being a hagiography, it is about as powerful a defense of Thatcher's record as is likely ever to be written."

In a review on *The Scotsman* Michael Fry argued that the book is an unremarkable, average account of the Thatcher years, but that it did have some redeeming qualities. He wrote: "Some of the books will be good and some bad. I would say this one comes about halfway in between. Berlinski shows commitment and energy as an author, beside an ability to wheedle great men into telling her things they might not have vouchsafed to anybody else."

Paul Sweeney of *The Irish Times* stated in his review of the biography that the timing of a positive biography on Margaret Thatcher was quite ironic, saying: "She says Thatcher was enormously significant. She is correct. She says she changed the world. She is correct. But when she says "for the better", she is very wrong." At the same time, Sweeney praises her ability to write, saying, "Yet Berlinski can write and she adopts an interesting style by reproducing interviews with some major players and observers of Thatcher's time. It gives a good insight into the person and her background."

Vincent Carroll wrote in *The Wall Street Journal* that "Despite Ms. Berlinski's obvious admiration for her subject," the book "is a pleasure to read in part because of its unflinching judgments." He continued, "As an interviewer herself, Ms. Berlinski is subtle and dogged. And while she never interviews Mrs. Thatcher, whose mind has reportedly been clouded by strokes, she does sit down with a number of figures from the Thatcher era -- both loyal insiders and antagonists like former Labour leader Neil Kinnock -- and the exchanges she selects rank among the book's highlights."

Peter Robinson described the book as "splendid" in the *National Review*, describing it as "a very fine volume--brisk, engrossing, insightful, often charming, and almost always rigorous." In answering the question, "Why Thatcher? Why was it she who understood that something had to be done and then did it? Berlinski proves wonderful here, seeing past all the usual explanations." Berlinski's "single failing," is that "She devotes more than 300 pages to proving that Thatcher remade Britain, and, to a remarkable extent, the world. Then she can't bring herself to admit it."

John R. Coyne Jr. concluded his positive review in *the Washington Times* by noting of Thatcher that "an attractive, articulate, intelligent and single-minded woman with a political purpose has a natural advantage over her male counterparts, who frequently can be persuaded to behave - or speak - in ways they wouldn't consider when dealing with other men. ... A corollary of this might be that an attractive, articulate, intelligent and single-minded woman with a literary purpose - and a recorder - frequently can persuade old male adversaries of Margaret Thatcher - especially verbose old Laborite Neil Kinnock - to run on in ways they might later regret - but that readers of this fresh, original and extremely well-written book will greatly appreciate."

Source (edited): "http://en.wikipedia.org/wiki/There_Is_No_Alternative:_Why_Margaret_Thatcher_Matters"

There is no alternative

There is no alternative (shortened as **TINA**) was a slogan which Margaret Thatcher, the conservative British Prime Minister used often. In economics, politics, and political economy, it has come to mean that "there is no alternative" to the status quo of their economic system and economic liberalism. This is the main slogan of economic liberalism, arguing that free markets, free trade, and capitalist globalization are the only way in which modern societies can go, as any deviation from their doctrine is certain to lead to disaster.

The phrase may be traced to its emphatic use by nineteenth-century libertarian thinker Herbert Spencer.

In the early nineties, Francis Fukuyama wrote a book named *The End of History and the Last Man*, which in a similar strain argued that liberal democracy had triumphed over communism and the historical struggle between political systems was over (though there could still be future events).

This phrase is also the company slogan for a printing company established in 2002 in Schaumburg, Illinois called M13 Graphics.

Source (edited): "http://en.wikipedia.org/wiki/There_is_no_alternative"

United Kingdom general election, 1979

The **United Kingdom general election of 1979** was held on 3 May 1979 to elect 635 members to the British House of Commons. The Conservative Party, led by Margaret Thatcher ousted the incumbent Labour government of James Callaghan with a parliamentary majority of 43 seats. The election was the first of four consecutive election victories for the Conservative Party, and Margaret Thatcher became the United Kingdom's - and Europe's - first female head of government.

James Callaghan's Labour government had lost its parliamentary majority during the 1974-79 parliament, and had had to make agreements with the Liberals, the Ulster Unionists, as well as the Scottish and Welsh nationalists. When the Scottish Nationalists withdrew support, a vote of no confidence was passed on Callaghan's government, triggering a general election.

The Labour campaign was hampered by the series of industrial disputes and strikes during the Winter of 1978-79, now referred to as the Winter of Discontent and the party focussed it's campaign on support for the National Health Service and full employment. The Conservative campaign employed the advertising agency Saatchi & Saatchi and pledged to control inflation as well as curbing the power of the trade unions. The Liberal Party was damaged by allegations that it's former leader Jeremy Thorpe had been involved in a homosexual affair and had conspired to commit murder.

The election saw a 5.2% swing from Labour to the Conservatives, the largest swing since 1945. Margaret Thatcher became Prime Minister, and Callaghan was replaced as Labour leader by Michael Foot in 1980. Results for the election were broadcast live on the BBC, and presented by David Dimbleby, Robert McKenzie, David Butler and Robin Day.

Background

Callaghan had succeeded Harold Wilson as Labour Prime Minister after the latter's surprise resignation in April 1976. By March 1977 Labour's small 1974 majority had become a minority government after several by-election defeats, and from March 1977 to August 1978 Callaghan governed by an agreement with the Liberal Party through the Lib-Lab pact. Callaghan then considered calling an election in the autumn of 1978 but ultimately decided that a possible economic upturn in 1979 could favour his party at the polls.

However, events would soon overtake the Labour government. A series of industrial disputes in the winter of 1978-79, dubbed the "Winter of Discontent", led to widespread strikes across the country and seriously hurt Labour's standings in the polls. When the Scottish National Party (SNP) withdrew support for the Scotland Act 1978, a vote of no confidence was held and passed by one vote on 28 March 1979, forcing Callaghan to either resign or call a general election. As the previous election had been held in October 1974, Labour could have held on until the autumn of 1979 if it had not been for the lost confidence vote.

Margaret Thatcher had won her party's 1975 leadership election over former leader Edward Heath.

David Steel had replaced Jeremy Thorpe as leader of the Liberal Party in 1976, after accusations of homosexuality and allegations of a conspiracy to commit murder forced Thorpe to resign (see Rinkagate). The scandals led to a fall in the Liberal vote after what was thought to be a breakthrough in the February 1974 election.

Campaign

This was the first election since 1959 to feature 3 new leaders for the main political parties. The three main parties all advocated cutting income tax. Labour and the Conservatives did not specify the exact thresholds of income tax they would implement but the Liberals did, claiming they would have income tax starting at 20% with a top rate of 50%.

The Labour campaign reiterated their support for the National Health Service and full employment and focused on the damage they believed the Conservatives would do to the country. In an early campaign broadcast, Callaghan asked: "The question you will have to consider is whether we risk tearing everything up by the roots". Towards the end of Labour's campaign Callaghan claimed a Conservative government "would sit back and just allow firms to go bankrupt and jobs to be lost in the middle of a world recession" and that the Conservatives were "too big a gamble to take".

The Conservatives campaigned on economic issues, pledging to control inflation and to reduce the increasing power of the unions who supported the mass strikes. They also employed the advertising agency Saatchi & Saatchi. The Conservative campaign was focused on gaining support from traditional Labour voters who had never voted Conservative before, first-time voters and people who had voted Liberal in 1974. Mrs. Thatcher's advisers, Gordon Reece and Timothy Bell, co-ordinated their presentation with the editor of *The Sun*, Larry Lamb. *The Sun* printed a series of articles by disillusioned former Labour ministers (Reginald Prentice, Richard Marsh, Lord George-Brown, Alfred Robens and Lord Chalfont) detailing why they had switched their support to Mrs Thatcher. She explicitly asked Labour voters for their support when she launched her campaign in Cardiff, claiming that Labour was now extreme. An analysis of the election claimed that the Conservatives gained an 11% swing among the skilled working-class (the C2s) and a 9% swing amongst the unskilled working class (the DEs).

Results

In the end, the overall swing of 5.2% was the largest since 1945 and gave the Conservatives a workable majority of 43 for the country's first female Prime Minister. The Conservative victory in 1979 also marked a change in government which would continue for 18 years until the Labour victory in 1997. The SNP saw a massive collapse in support, losing 9 of their 11 MPs to the three main political parties alike. The Liberals had a disappointing night, as they were affected by the scandal involving former Liberal leader Jeremy Thorpe. Thorpe lost his seat in North Devon to the Conservatives.

All parties shown.
N.B. The Vanguard Progressive Unionist Party had folded in 1978. Of its three MPs, two joined the Ulster Unionist Party (one held his seat, the other lost to the Democratic Unionist Party) and the third defended and held his seat for the United Ulster Unionist Party.

James Kilfedder had been previously elected as an Ulster Unionist MP, but left the party, defending and holding his seat as an Independent Ulster Unionist. He subsequently founded the Ulster Popular Unionist Party but did not use that label in this election.

Votes summary

Seats summary

Source (edited): "http://en.wikipedia.org/wiki/United_Kingdom_general_election,_1979"

United Kingdom general election, 1983

The **1983 United Kingdom general election** was held on 9 June 1983. It gave the Conservative Party under Margaret Thatcher the most decisive election victory since that of Labour in 1945.

The opposition vote split almost evenly between the SDP/Liberal Alliance and Labour. With its worst performance since 1918, the Labour vote fell by over 3 million from 1979 and this accounted for both a national swing of almost 4% towards the Conservatives and their larger parliamentary majority of 144, even though the Conservatives' total vote fell by almost 700,000.

Mrs Thatcher's first four years as prime minister had not been an easy time. Unemployment had rocketed in the first three years of her term as she battled to control inflation that had ravaged Britain for most of the 1970s. By the start of 1982, unemployment had passed the 3,000,000 mark - for the first time since before the Second World War - and the economy had been in recession for nearly two years. However, British victory in the Falklands War later that year sparked a dramatic rise in Tory popularity, and as Mrs Thatcher's new found popularity continued in 1983 the Tories were most people's firm favourites to win the election.

The SDP-Liberal Alliance polled only a few votes behind the Labour Party but received considerably fewer seats. The Alliance gained over 25% of the popular vote, the largest such percentage for any third party since the 1923 general election. The Liberals argued that a proportional electoral system would have given them a more representative number of MPs. Changing the electoral system had been a long-running Liberal Party campaign plank and would later be adopted by the Liberal Democrats.

Labour leader Michael Foot, who had been at the helm since the resignation of James Callaghan (prime minister from 1976 to 1979) in late 1980, resigned soon after the election and was succeeded by Neil Kinnock. Although the election was one of the party's worst, the new crop of MPs included two future Labour Prime Ministers, Tony Blair and Gordon Brown.

The election night was broadcast live on the BBC, and was presented by Peter Snow, David Dimbleby and Robin Day.

Background and campaign

Michael Foot was elected leader of the Labour party in 1980, replacing James Callaghan. The election of Foot signalled that the core of the party was swinging to the left and the move exacerbated divisions within the party. In 1981 a group of senior figures including Roy Jenkins, David Owen, Bill Rodgers and Shirley Williams left Labour to found the Social Democratic Party (SDP). The SDP agreed to a pact with the Liberals for the 1983 elections and stood as The Alliance.

The campaign displayed the huge divisions between the two major parties. Thatcher had been extremely unpopular during her first two years in office until the swift and decisive victory in the Falklands War, coupled with an improving economy, considerably raised her standings in the polls. The Conservatives' key issues included employment, economic growth, and defence. Labour's campaign manifesto involved leaving the European Economic Community, abolishing the House of Lords, abandoning the United Kingdom's nuclear deterrent by cancelling Trident and removing cruise missiles — a policy programme dubbed by Labour MP Gerald Kaufman as "the longest suicide note in history". "Although, at barely 37 pages, it only seemed interminable", noted Roy Hattersley. Pro-Labour political journalist Michael White, writing in

The Guardian, commented, "There was something magnificently brave about Michael Foot's campaign — but it was like the Battle of the Somme."

National election, 1979

Following boundary changes in 1983, the BBC and ITN (Independent Television News) co-produced a calculation of how the 1979 general election would have gone if fought on the new 1983 boundaries. The following table shows the effects of the boundary changes on the House of Commons:

The Prime Minister Margaret Thatcher visited Buckingham Palace on the afternoon of 9 May and asked the Queen to dissolve Parliament on 13 May, announcing that the election would be held on 9 June. The key dates were as follows:

Results

The election saw a landslide victory for the Conservatives, achieving their best results since 1959. Although there was a slight drop in their share of the vote, they made significant gains at the expense of Labour. The night was a disaster for the Labour party, their share of the vote fell by over 9%, which meant they were only 700,000 votes ahead of the newly formed 3rd party the SDP-Liberal Alliance. The massive increase of support for the Alliance at the expense of Labour meant that, in many seats, the collapse in the Labour vote allowed the Conservatives to win. Despite winning over 25% of the national vote, however, the Alliance got less than 4% of seats - 186 fewer than Labour.

The most notable loss of the night was Tony Benn, who lost his seat in Bristol East. SDP President Shirley Williams, a prominent leader of the Social Democratic party, lost her Crosby seat which she had won in a by-election in 1981. Bill Rodgers, another leader of the Alliance (One of the "Gang of Four") also failed to win his old seat that had held as a Labour MP.

All parties with more than 500 votes shown.

N.B. The SDP-Liberal Alliance vote is compared with the Liberal Party vote in the 1979 election.

The Independent Unionist elected in the 1979 election defended and held his seat for the Ulster Popular Unionist Party. The United Ulster Unionist Party dissolved and its sole MP did not re-stand.

The Independent Republican elected in the 1979 election died in 1981. In the ensuring by-election the seat was won by Bobby Sands, an Anti-H-Block/Armagh Political Prisoner who then died and was succeeded by an Anti-H-Block Proxy Political Prisoner candidate Owen Carron. He defended and lost his seat standing for Sinn Féin who contested seats in Northern Ireland for the first time since 1959.

This election was fought under revised boundaries. The changes reflect those comparing to the notional results on the new boundaries. One significant change was the increase in the number of seats allocated to Northern Ireland from 12 to 17.

Votes summary

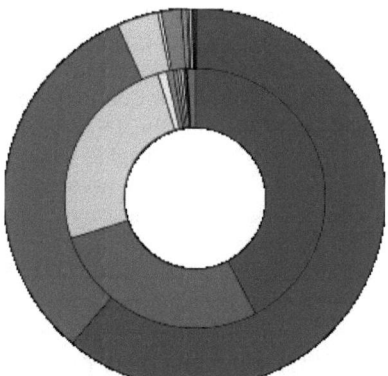

Seats won in the election (outer ring) against number of votes (inner ring).

Seats summary

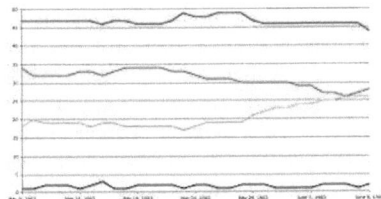

Data from Guardian daily polls published in *The Guardian* between May and June 1983
Colour Key: BLUE Conservative, RED Labour, ORANGE Alliance, BLACK Others

1983 UK General Election				
Party	% of votes	% of seats	difference	difference squared
Conservative	42.3	61.1	18.8	353.44
Labour	27.6	32.2	4.6	21.16
SDP-Liberal Alliance	25.4	3.5	-21.9	479.61
SNP	1.1	0.3	-0.8	0.64
Ulster Unionist	0.8	1.7	0.9	0.81
Democratic Unionist	0.5	0.5	0	0
SDLP	0.4	0.2	-0.2	0.04
Plaid Cymru	0.4	0.3	-0.1	0.01
Sinn Fein	0.3	0.2	-0.1	0.01
Alliance	0.2	0	-0.2	0.04
Ecology	0.2	0	-0.2	0.04
Independent	0.1	0	-0.1	0.01
National Front	0.1	0	-0.1	0.01
Ulster Popular	0.1	0.2	0.1	0.01
Independent Labour	0.1	0	-0.1	0.01
		Total		855.84
		Halved		427.92
		Square Root		20.69

The disproportionality of the house of parliament in the 1983 election was 20.69 according to the Gallagher Index, mainly between the Conservatives and SDP-Liberal Alliance.

Labour targets

In order to regain an overall majority, Labour needed to make at least 65 gains.
Source (edited): "http://en.wikipedia.org/wiki/United_Kingdom_general_election,_1983"

United Kingdom general election, 1987

The **United Kingdom general election of 1987** was held on 11 June 1987, to elect 650 members to the British House of Commons. The election was the third consecutive election victory for the Conservative Party under the leadership of Margaret Thatcher, who became the first Prime Minister since the 2nd Earl of Liverpool to lead a party into three successive election victories.

The Conservatives ran a campaign focusing on lower taxes, a strong economy and defence. They also emphasised that unemployment had fallen below 3 million for the first time since 1981, and inflation was standing at 4%, its lowest level for many years. The tabloid media also had strong support for the Conservatives, particularly *The Sun*, which ran anti-Labour articles with headlines such as: *Why I'm backing Kinnock, by Stalin*. The Labour Party, led by Neil Kinnock was slowly moving towards a more centrist policy platform. The main aim of the Labour party was, arguably, not to win a majority of parliamentary seats but simply to re-establish themselves as the main progressive centre-left alternative to the Conservatives, after the rise of the SDP forced Labour onto the defence. Indeed, the Labour party succeeded in doing so with this general election. The Alliance between the Social Democratic Party and the Liberal Party was renewed but co-leaders David Owen and David Steel could not agree whether to support either major party in the event of a hung parliament.

The Conservatives were returned to government, having suffered a net loss of only 21 seats, leaving them with 376 MPs. Labour succeeded in resisting challenge by the SPD-Liberal Alliance to replace them as the main opposition, and managed to increase their vote share in Scotland, Wales and Northern England. However, Labour still returned only 229 MPs to Westminster. The election was a disappointment for the SDP-Liberal Alliance, who saw their vote share fall and suffered a net loss of one seat as well as former SDP leader Roy Jenkins losing his seat. This led to the two parties eventually merging completely to become the Liberal Democrats. In Northern Ireland, the main unionist parties maintained their alliance in opposition to the Anglo-Irish Agreement, however the Ulster Unionists lost two seats to the Social Democratic and Labour Party. The election night was covered live on the BBC, and presented by David Dimbleby, Peter Snow, and Robin Day.

Campaign and policies

The Conservatives' campaign emphasized lower taxes, a strong economy, and defence, and also employed rapid-response reactions to take advantage of Labour errors. Norman Tebbit and Saatchi and Saatchi spearheaded the Conservative campaign. However, when on 'Wobbly Thursday' it was rumoured a Marplan opinion poll showed a 2% Conservative lead, the 'exiles' camp of David Young, Tim Bell and the Young and Rubicam firm advocated a more aggressively anti-Labour message. This was when, according to Young's memoirs, Young got Tebbit by the lapels and shook him, shouting: "Norman, listen to me, we're about to lose this fucking election". In his memoirs Tebbit defends the Conservative campaign: "We finished exactly as planned on the ground where Labour was weak and we were strong – defence, taxation, and the economy". During the election campaign however Tebbit and Thatcher argued.

Bell and Saatchi and Saatchi produced memorable posters for the Conservatives, such as a picture of a British soldier's arms raised in surrender with the caption: "Labour's Policy On Arms"—a reference to Labour's policy of unilateral nuclear disarmament. The first Conservative party political broadcast played on the theme of "Freedom" and ended with a fluttering Union Jack, the hymn *I Vow to Thee, My Country* and the slogan: "It's Great To Be Great Again".

The Labour campaign was a marked change from previous efforts; professionally directed by Peter Mandelson and Bryan Gould, it concentrated on presenting and improving Neil Kinnock's image to the electorate. Labour's first party political broadcast, dubbed *Kinnock: The Movie*, was directed by Hugh Hudson of *Chariots of Fire* fame, and concentrated on portraying Kinnock as a caring, compassionate family man. He was particularly critical of the high unemployment that the Tory government's economic policies had resulted in, as well as condemning the wait for treatment that many patients had endured on the National Health Service. Kinnock's personal popularity jumped 16 points overnight after the initial broadcast.

On 24 May, Kinnock was interviewed by David Frost and claimed that Labour's alternative defence strategy in the event of a Soviet attack would be "using the resources you've got to make any occupation totally untenable". In a speech two days later Mrs. Thatcher attacked Labour's defence policy as a programme for "defeat, surrender, occupation, and finally, prolonged guerrilla fighting...I do not understand how anyone who aspires to Government can treat the defence of our country so lightly."

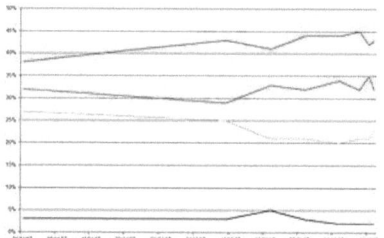

Data from Guardian daily polls published in *The Guardian* between April and June 1987
Colour Key: BLUE Conservative, RED Labour, ORANGE SDP-Liberal Alliance, BLACK Others

Results

The Conservatives were returned with a comfortable majority, down slightly on 1983 with a swing of 1.5% towards Labour. Increasing polarisation marked divisions across the country: the Conservatives dominated southern England and took additional seats from Labour in the south but performed less well in Northern England, Scotland, and Wales. Yet the overall result of this election proved that the policies of Margaret Thatcher retained significant support, with the Conservatives given a third convincing majority.

Despite initial optimism and the professional campaign run by Neil Kinnock, the election brought only twenty additional seats for Labour from the 1983 Conservative landslide. In many southern areas, the Labour vote actually fell, with the party losing seats in London. However, it represented a decisive victory against the SDP–Liberal Alliance and marked out the Labour Party as the main opposition to the Conservative Party. This was in stark contrast to 1983, when the Labour Party and the SDP–Liberal Alliance took a roughly equal share of the vote.

The result for the SDP–Liberal Alliance was a disappointment, in that they had hoped to overtake Labour as the second party in the UK in terms of vote share. Instead, they lost one net seat and saw their vote share drop by almost 3%, with a widening gap of 8% between them and the Labour party (compared to a 2% gap four years before). These results would eventually lead to the end of the SDP–Liberal Alliance and the birth of the Liberal Democrats.

Most of the prominent MPs retained their seats. Notable failures included Enoch Powell and two SDP–Liberal Alliance members, Liberal Clement Freud and former SDP leader Roy Jenkins.

In Northern Ireland, the various unionist parties maintained an electoral pact (with a few dissenters) in opposition to the Anglo-Irish Agreement. However, the Ulster Unionist lost two seats to the Social Democratic and Labour Party.

All parties gaining over 500 votes listed.

Votes summary

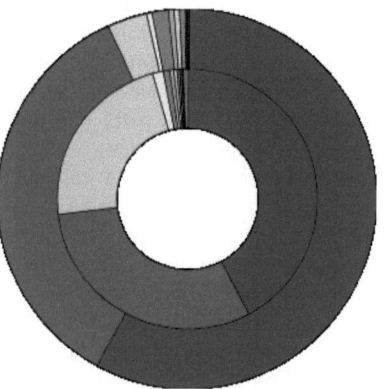

Seats won in the election (outer ring) against number of votes (inner ring).

Seats summary

Source (edited): "http://en.wikipedia.org/wiki/United_Kingdom_general_election,_1987"

University of Buckingham

The **University of Buckingham** (UB) is an independent, non-sectarian research and teaching university located in Buckingham, Buckinghamshire, England, on the banks of the River Great Ouse. Buckingham's funding regime is not like that of other UK universities, but rather is on the model of many US universities, as it does not receive direct state funding. Prior to the American-owned BPP University College of Professional Studies gaining university college status in 2010, Buckingham was Britain's only privately-funded university. Buckingham offers bachelor's degrees, master's degrees, and doctoral degrees through five schools of study.

The 'Schools' (or Faculties) of Law and Science are situated in the upper campus; the river-side campus covers Humanities, Business, Social Sciences, Biomedical science, and Education. As the University is expanding, it has acquired a new site on the west side of the river, hence increasing the capacity of the river-side campus as a whole. Teaching on some master's degrees takes place in London, in Grosvenor Place, at the home of one its partner institutions: the European School of Economics. Prominent academics include: philosopher Roger Scruton, philosopher and educationalist Anthony O'Hear, educationalist Alan Smithers, the former Chief Inspector of Schools Chris Woodhead, the cancer specialist Karol Sikora, the historian and political scientist Geoffrey Alderman, and the expert in UK Intelligence Anthony Glees.

History

Some of the founding academics migrated from the University of Oxford, disillusioned or wary of aspects of the late 1960s' ethos. On 27 May 1967, *The Times* published a letter from Dr J. W. Paulley, which said: "Is it now time to examine the possibility of creating at least one university in this country on the pattern of [the] great private foundations in the USA". Three London conferences followed which explored this idea.

Subsequently the university was incorporated as the University College of Buckingham in 1976, and received its Royal Charter from the Queen in 1983.

Its development was influenced by the libertarian Institute of Economic Affairs, in particular, Harry Ferns and Ralph Harris, heads of the Institute. In keeping with its adherence to a libertarian philosophy, the university's foundation-stone was laid by Margaret Thatcher, who was also to be the university's Chancellor (nominal and ceremonial head) between 1993 and 1998. The University's first three Vice-Chancellors were Lord Beloff (1913–1999), former Gladstone Professor of Politics at the University of Oxford; Sir Alan Peacock, the economist, founder of the Economics department at the University of York, and Fellow of the British Academy; and Sir Richard Luce, now Lord Luce, the former Minister for the Arts.

Teaching

The University's four schools are Law, Humanities, Business, and Science and Medicine. Each of these is presided over by a Dean.

One feature of the University that has attracted notice is its continuation of the tradition of "tutorial" teaching (i.e. very small group teaching) which its founders brought over from the University of Oxford. While there are seminars and lectures, much of the teaching is done in small groups of 4 to 8 students, with one member of staff. The staff-student ratio is 1:7.8, which is high among UK universities. The Times Good University Guide (2009) notes that "one-to-one tutorials, which have almost died out elsewhere, with the exception of Oxbridge...are quite common at Buckingham".

The quality of the University's provision is maintained, as at other UK universities, by an external examiner system (i.e., professors from other universities oversee and report on exams and marking), by an academic advisory council (comprising a range of subject-specialist academics from other universities), and by membership of the Quality Assurance Agency for Higher Education (QAA).

The Department of Education has two aspects, research and vocational: it conducts research into education and school provision (see above), and also maintains various PGCE courses, for teacher training. The Department of Education is home to some of the most prominent educationalists in Britain, including Professor Chris Woodhead (former head of Ofsted), Professor Anthony O'Hear (director of the Royal Institute of Philosophy), and Professor Alan Smithers. Its postgraduate certificate in education – which deals with both the state and the independent sector – is accredited with Qualified Teacher Status which means that it also qualifies graduates to teach in the state sector.

The University was created as a liberal arts college, and the major humanities subjects such as history and politics are offered with economics as a degree in international studies. Economics, however, is available as a stand-alone degree. So too is English literature, as a single honours subject, and in combinations with English Language, or Journalism, and related areas. The Professor of Economics, and Dean of Humanities, Professor Martin Ricketts, is the chair of the Institute of Economic Affairs Academic Advisory Council.

Some degree programmes at Buckingham, Law for example, place greater emphasis on exams as an assessment method rather than coursework, but in general its degree programmes balance assessment between exams and coursework.

School of Medicine

The cancer specialist Karol Sikora is Dean of the School of Medicine. The School offers postgraduate MD programmes for qualified doctors in a range of specialisations, but is not approved by the General Medical Council as it does not yet offer an undergraduate medical qualification (Bachelor of Medicine, Bachelor of Surgery).

The School had an association with the alternative medicine community via a Diploma course in integrated medicine. This was later withdrawn under pressure from David Colquhoun, a campaigner against alternative medicine. Karol Sikora is a Foundation Fellow of Prince Charles' now-defunct alternative medicine lobby group the Foundation for Integrated Health and Chair of the

Faculty of Integrated Medicine, which is unaffiliated with any university but also includes Drs Rosy Daniel and Mark Atkinson, who co-ordinated Buckingham's "integrated medicine" course. Daniel has been criticised by David Colquhoun for breaches of the Cancer Act 1939, regarding claims she made for *Carctol*, a herbal remedy. Prof. Andrew Miles is on the scientific council of the *College of Medicine* an alternative medicine lobby group linked to the Prince of Wales. Karol Sikora is also a "professional member" of this organisation.

Sikora is very critical of cancer care available on the National Health Service. During President Obama's campaign for healthcare reform, he appeared in a Republican Party attack ad in the United States criticising the NHS. The ad led Imperial College to seek legal advice to stop Sikora from claiming to be a professor of cancer medicine at Imperial; a claim that he had made repeatedly over the previous five years.

Professor of Theoretical Medicine at the school is Bruce Charlton, controversial editor of the journal Medical hypotheses, who has recently been dismissed as editor by publisher Elsevier over the publication of a paper by AIDS denialists claiming that HIV is not responsible for AIDS and concerns over the lack of peer-review at the journal.

Degrees: timescale and cost

The university offers traditional degrees over a shorter time-frame. Students at Buckingham study for eight terms over two years, rather than nine terms over three, which (with extra teaching) fits a three-year degree into two years. From September 2009, tuition fees for full-time UK and EU undergraduate students will be £8,040 per year for these two-year Bachelor's degree programmes. For non-EU students, fees will be equivalent to £13,500 p.a. Because Buckingham's degrees take only two years to complete, the university views its courses as cost-effective compared to ordinary UK university courses, once living expenses and the income from an extra year's employment are taken into account.

Dr Terence Kealey, published an article on 4 June in the *Daily Telegraph* newspaper arguing that getting better-funded and more effective universities means charging higher fees.

League tables
UK ranking

The University was ranked 27th out of 115 universities in *Times Higher Education's* "Table of Tables" 2010.

In 2010, *The Independent*, in association with its *Complete University Guide 2010-11*, ranked Buckingham as the 20th best university out of 115 institutions in the UK. The *Sunday Times* University guide for 2010 included Buckingham in its league tables in 48th position out of 122 UK higher education institutes stating that: "we rank the private University of Buckingham for the first time in our main league table this year. Top for student satisfaction, with the lowest level of graduate unemployment, the best student/staff ratio and the lowest drop-out rate compared to benchmark. Buckingham makes quite an entrance ..." Confusingly, the same publisher does not include Buckingham in its Good University Guide because Buckingham receives no state funding and therefore does not participate in the government's Research Assessment Exercise, which forms part of the *Times* ranking criteria (but not the *Sunday Times*). For this same reason, Buckingham may be absent from other rankings based on, or which require, this measure.

Times Higher Education reported that the University's 2008 graduates had the highest employment rate after six months.

In recent years the University has consistently ranked highly in student satisfaction surveys. For example, Times Higher Education reported that Buckingham was ranked first in 2006, 2007 and 2008 in the NSS or National Student Survey of student satisfaction. This is a census, albeit controversial, of final-year undergraduates conducted by IposMori, the polling organisation, to determine satisfaction levels at UK universities. The survey relates to the whole student experience, from the experience of classes, and lecturer feedback, to the quality of pastoral care. In 2009, the University of Buckingham dropped to second place and in 2010 returned to first place.

Department rankings

The league tables of individual university departments in *The Guardian University Guide 2010*, produced by *The Guardian* newspaper, ranked English at Buckingham as 15th out of 97 UK departments, Business as 20th out of 113 departments, and Law as 23rd out of 89 departments. The updating of these league tables, in *The Guardian University Guide 2011*, ranks Business as the second-best department in the UK, English as the 6th, and Law as the 24th.

Global ranking

As of 2009, the university does not rank in the top 600 universities globally as rated by Quacquarelli Symonds and *Times Higher Education*; nor does it rank in the top 500 universities rated by the Academic Ranking of World Universities in 2010. However, it is ranked at 4,420 in the 2010 Webometrics Ranking of World Universities.

Quality

The University's Royal Charter, unlike those of other universities, provides for three sovereign bodies, the third one (in addition to the usual Council and Senate) being the Academic Advisory Council, which is a group of external academics that audits the academic staff.

When the national Quality Assurance Agency (QAA) was created, the University felt it should join, even though - as Britain's only independent University – it is markedly different from the state-funded universities that the QAA otherwise audits.

The University has emerged as a critic of the QAA. Professor Geoffrey Alderman, in his inaugural lecture at the University of Buckingham *Teaching Quality Assessment, League Tables and the Decline of Academic Standards in*

British Higher Education demonstrated that degree inflation had taken off in the 10 years of the QAA's existence. This lecture provoked a wide national debate which encouraged the House of Commons Select Committee to review quality and related issues.

The University got "broad confidence" (the highest band) in its first QAA audit in 2003. In 2008 the QAA said that:
"limited confidence can reasonably be placed in the soundness of the University's current and likely future management of the academic standards of its awards" and also that "confidence can reasonably be placed in the soundness of the University's current and likely future management of the quality of the learning opportunities available to students."
The University's Vice-Chancellor, Dr Terence Kealey, commented on the QAA report in the Times Higher Education magazine on 16 September 2008, followed a week later by a lead letter from the Chief Executive of the QAA and an article by Melanie Newman in the same issue.

A few weeks later, Dr Kealey discussed the QAA in a feature article in the Guardian newspaper. A week later the Chief Executive of QAA and Professor Gill Evans responded in the same paper. The Vice-Chancellor, Dr Terence Kealey, then wrote a further article for the Guardian newspaper linking the QAA inspection regime with degree inflation which has so undermined UK Higher Education that the Burgess Report recommends abandoning classed degrees altogether.

In June 2009 Dr Kealey wrote a further article, published on 4 June in The Independent newspaper, arguing that the QAA should be incorporated into Hefce and a new Standards Assurance Agency should be set up.

The University's criticisms of QAA and of the regulatory regime have been endorsed by the House of Commons Select Committee as discussed in The Times newspaper by Professor Geoffrey Alderman on 4 August 2009.

Alumni and honorary graduates

Honorary graduates include: the Rt Hon Frank Field, the Labour MP; Sir Steven Redgrave, the Olympic oarsman; Baroness Noakes, the Conservative politician (opponent of Identity cards); Sir Stuart Hampson, former head of the John Lewis Partnership; Sir Christopher Ondaatje, the publisher, writer, and philanthropist; and the journalist Charles Moore; Baronness Helena Kennedy, the distinguished barrister; and Nigel Lawson, Lord Lawson of Blaby, former Chancellor of the Exchequer.

Prominent alumni include: Bader Ben Hirsi, Susanne Klatten, Michael Misick, Brandon Lewis, Olagunsoye Oyinlola, Mark Lancaster, the MP for Milton Keynes North and Graham Roos who, since 2011, has been appointed the University's first Creative Artist in Residence.

Prominent international alumni include Pravind Jugnauth MP in the Mauritius parliament, former Deputy Prime Minister, and the Leader of one of Mauritius's main parties, the Militant Socialist Movement.

In the BBC Radio 4 panel game *The Museum of Curiosity*, host John Lloyd claims to be, "The Professor of Ignorance at the University of Buckingham".

Author V. M. Xavier presented special cultural performances at student functions in the 1980s.

External degrees

The University awards undergraduate and graduate (Masters/MBA) degrees to students who have studied at the European School of Economics and at the Sarajevo School of Science and Technology.

Chancellorship

The immediate past- Chancellor is Sir Martin Jacomb, Chairman of Canary Wharf Group PLC, and Share PLC (in Aylesbury), and the director of other companies including Oxford Playhouse Trust. He was Chairman of Prudential PLC from 1995 to 2000 and last year retired from the boards of Rio Tinto Group and Marks & Spencer. Former Chancellors of the university have been Margaret Thatcher who retired in 1999, and Lord Hailsham of St Marylebone.

Lord Tanlaw was appointed to succeed Sir Martin as Chancellor in May 2010.

The current Vice-Chancellor is Dr Terence Kealey, formerly of the Department of Clinical Biochemistry at Cambridge University, who has held the post since April 2001. Kealey is known for his research challenging the idea that education and science are public goods needing public subsidies. He wrote an academic book on the subject in 1996 The Economic Laws of Scientific Research which he repackaged and updated for a general audience in 2008 as Sex, Science and Profits.

Kealey sparked a sexism row in September 2009. The *Times Higher Education* had commissioned, for its issue of 17 September 2009, seven articles of 500 words each on the seven deadly sins of academia. The seven sins were *sartorial inelegance, procrastination, snobbery, lust, arrogance, complacency* and *pedantry,* and the commissioning editor, Matthew Reisz, wrote that the contributors "entered into the spirit and offered amusing examples of their sins in action …". The illustrations in the magazine reflected the humour of the feature. Kealey wrote on *lust,* and he adopted a satirical tone, claiming that young female students were a "perk" for male academics and they should "look but not touch". Over the next week the *Times Higher Education* website filled with comments about the article, many expressing shock but some expressing support. On 23 September the London Daily Telegraph ran a story about the article and the backlash was swift from academics. Kealey was criticised by the University and College Union and the National Union of Students who said his comments displayed an "astounding lack of respect for women". At the same time Kealey was defended by scholars such as Professor Mary Beard of Cambridge University who in her online blog for the *Times* newspaper wrote that it was instantly clear that the piece was satire. Kealey wrote a defence of his piece in the Daily Telegraph and he was also defended by the editor of the THE but nonetheless he wrote a piece in the Times Education Supplement three weeks later in which he said that it is a mistake for a scholar to write ambiguously, which must generally preclude the use of satire, irony, humour or parody in academic writing.

In February 2010, Kealey proposed the establishment of a new independent university, modelled on American liberal arts colleges, that would concentrate on undergraduate teaching rather than research. The plan is currently being considered by the Headmasters' and Headmistresses' Conference (HMC), whose 243 members include independent schools such as Eton, Winchester and St Paul's. Kealey believes that complaints about impersonal teaching and oversized classes at many traditional universities mean there will be strong demand for higher education with staff-student ratios similar to that provided by independent secondary schools.

University of Buckingham Press

The University of Buckingham Press publishes in the areas of law, education, and business through its journal articles, books, reports and other material. In 2006 the press relaunched The Denning Law Journal and it is now available in print and its whole archive is online. It also publishes three other journals: The Buckingham Journal of Language and Linguistics, The Journal of Prediction Markets, and The Journal of Gambling Business and Economics. It has a co-publishing arrangement with The Policy Exchange for its Foundations series.

The university has close links with colleges abroad including the Sarajevo School of Science and Technology, an independent university college in Bosnia and Herzegovina. Teaching takes place in Sarajevo. After completing a bachelor's degree, master's degree or PhD students receive a diploma from both universities.

Source (edited): "http://en.wikipedia.org/wiki/University_of_Buckingham"

Westland affair

The **Westland affair** was a political scandal for the British Conservative government of Margaret Thatcher in 1986. The argument was a result of differences of opinion within the government as to the future of the United Kingdom helicopter industry. The struggling Westland company, Britain's last helicopter manufacturer, was to be the subject of a rescue bid. While the Defence Secretary Michael Heseltine favoured a European solution, integrating Westland and British Aerospace (BAe) with Italian (Agusta) and French companies, the Prime Minister and the Trade and Industry Secretary Leon Brittan wanted to see Westland merge with Sikorsky, an American company. It resulted in Heseltine's resignation.

April 1985

The Westland affair originated with Alan Bristow's bid for the company in April 1985. By June Bristow was threatening to end his bid unless the Government assured him that there would be future orders for the company from the Ministry of Defence and that the repayment of over £40 million of launch aid for Westland's newest helicopter from the Department of Trade and Industry was waived. At a Government meeting it was decided that Norman Tebbit should persuade the Bank of England to cooperate with the main creditors in the hope that a recovery plan and new management would end the threat of receivership. Bristow withdrew his bid and Sir John Cuckney became chairman of Westland.

November 1985

Shortly thereafter an American company was thought to be preparing to bid for the company. Cuckney opposed this particular bid, as did Tebbit and Heseltine. Cuckney proposed that a new minority shareholder of 29.9% be introduced. No British firm was willing to enter this but an American company, Sikorsky, was interested. In November 1985 Sikorsky made an offer and Westland's management were favourable. Heseltine was opposed to this and called a conference of the National Armaments Directors (NAD) of Britain, France, Italy and West Germany to sign a document which would commit each country to only purchase helicopters designed and manufactured in Europe. If Westland went ahead with Sikorsky its helicopters, under this new agreement, would be unable to be bought by the four governments. Thatcher's and Leon Brittan's view was that it was up to Westland to decide which deal it wanted, and not the Government.

December 1985

Thatcher then convened two meetings to discuss Westland with Heseltine, Brittan, Tebbit, William Whitelaw, Geoffrey Howe and Nigel Lawson on 5 and 6 December. Brittan argued that NAD's opposition should be set aside, but Heseltine, Howe and Tebbit disagreed. Thatcher called a Cabinet meeting for 9 December, which Cuckney also attended to give a speech. Cuckney said that it was the management's view that the Sikorsky option was the best one. A majority of the Cabinet meeting agreed to dismiss NAD's opposition but Thatcher gave consent to both Heseltine and Brittan to explore a possible European deal which Westland's management could accept. She gave them until 4 pm on 13 December and if by then Westland rejected the European package, NAD's recommendations would be formally rejected. Westland chose Sikorsky instead of the European firms but Heseltine wanted another Cabinet meeting. Thatcher rejected his demands because Westland had made up its mind on which deal it would recommend.

At a Cabinet meeting on 12 December Heseltine, without warning, tried to discuss Westland but Thatcher was not willing to without the necessary papers. Heseltine was angry and claimed a meeting on Westland had been cancelled but Thatcher argued that no such meeting had ever been scheduled. Heseltine wanted his views on the alleged cancelled meeting to be included in the Cabinet minutes; it was not going to be mentioned until the Cabinet Secretary noticed they were absent, and added it himself.

Later, the European consortium came up with a new bid and Heseltine thought the Government's policy should be changed to enable the European bid to succeed. The disagreements between Brittan and Heseltine over Westland became public and were widely reported in the media.

January 1986

Westland's management were worried about future business with European governments and Thatcher replied to Cuckney to the effect that the British Government would continue to support it. Heseltine wanted to include less supportive views, but Thatcher did not allow this.

In early January Lloyds Bank sent Heseltine a letter and in Heseltine's reply he listed the things which in his view would happen if Westland chose Sikorsky instead of the European alternative. Heseltine claimed, contradicting Thatcher's reassurances to Cuckney, that Westland risked losing future European orders if the Sikorsky option was chosen. Heseltine leaked this letter to *The Times*. The letter, on Thatcher's request, was referred to the Solicitor-General, Patrick Mayhew. Mayhew sent a reply to Heseltine, noting "material inaccuracies" in Heseltine's letter. On 6 January Mayhew's letter was selectively leaked to the Press Association by the Chief Information Officer of the DTI, Colette Bowe on whose orders became a controversy. The Attorney-General, Sir Michael Havers, took a stern view of leaks and threatened to resign if an official inquiry was not set up to look into it. Thatcher agreed to do this.

A Cabinet meeting on Westland was scheduled for 9 January. Brittan and Heseltine both put forward their views. Thatcher concluded by saying that as this was a time of business negotiations all answers relating to Westland should be cleared through the Cabinet Office. Heseltine agreed. Nicholas Ridley intervened and asked whether this included not only future statements but repetition of past statements too. Thatcher gave an affirmative to both. Heseltine argued that he should be allowed to reaffirm statements he had already made but Thatcher disagreed, arguing that Cabinet collective responsibility should be observed. Heseltine was then said to have replied that there had been no collective responsibility in Westland. Peter Jenkins claims that Heseltine lost his cool, gathered his papers, got up from his chair and proclaimed "I can no longer be a member of this Cabinet" and then left the room. Heseltine then stormed out of Downing Street and announced his resignation to the assembled media. Within a few hours of his resignation, Heseltine produced a twenty-two minute statement of 2,500 words detailing his grievances. He blamed Thatcher's intransigence, saying his views were ignored. Thatcher sent a letter to Heseltine, as is customary on these occasions.

Thatcher then adjourned the Cabinet for a brief break. George Younger was then offered and accepted the office of Secretary of State for Defence, which Heseltine had just relinquished. The Prime Minister's office then requested Malcolm Rifkind to take up Younger's previous job, Secretary of State for Scotland, which he accepted. Cabinet then resumed. On 13 January Thatcher held a meeting with Whitelaw, Brittan, Younger and John Wakeham to decide what should then happen. The conclusion was that Brittan, rather than the Prime Minister, should reply to Heseltine's statement on that day. When in the House of Commons, Heseltine asked whether any letters from British Aerospace had been received. Brittan did receive a letter from BAe but it was marked *Private and Strictly Confidential* so he said in effect that he did not receive one. He was forced to return to the House a few hours later to apologise.

On 15 January there was a debate on Westland in the Commons in which Thatcher replied to Neil Kinnock, the leader of the Labour Party. Thatcher listed all the ministerial, committee and Cabinet meetings on Westland. Heseltine then made a speech criticising the way collective responsibility had been damaged over Westland.

Sir Robert Armstrong, the Cabinet Secretary, held an inquiry into the leaking of Mayhew's letter and reported his findings to the Prime Minister on 21 January. Armstrong concluded that Brittan had told Bowe to leak Mayhew's letter through a telephone conversation to Roger Mogg, Brittan's private secretary. Thatcher is said to have asked Brittan four times: "Leon, why didn't you tell me." Havers, who demanded the inquiry, later claimed: "Unless the PM is the most marvellous actress I've ever seen in my life she was as shocked as anybody that in fact it was on Leon Brittan's instructions."

On 23 January Thatcher had to make a speech to the Commons on Armstrong's inquiry. A meeting of the 1922 Committee, Conservative backbenchers, demanded Brittan's resignation. On 24 January therefore Brittan resigned because "it has become clear to me that I no longer command the full confidence of my colleagues."

On 27 January Labour set down an adjournment motion. Whitelaw, Howe, Wakeham, John Biffen and Douglas Hurd helped Thatcher draft her speech for this occasion. Ronald Millar, one of the Prime Minister's friends, was asked to help revise the speech and Thatcher remarked to him that she might cease to be Prime Minister by six o'clock that evening if things went bad. Neil Kinnock, the leader of the Opposition, was generally thought to have made a poor opening speech. Alan Clark recorded in his diary that "For a few seconds Kinnock had her cornered...But then he had an attack of wind, gave her time to recover." Heseltine was frustrated at Kinnock's failure to exploit the moment and claimed that Thatcher's statement brought "the politics of the matter to an end" and that he would support the

Government in the lobby.

Subsequent events

Heseltine's wish to see a strong European competitor has emerged in the form of the Eurocopter group and Agusta eventually merged with Westland in 2000 and then acquired GKN's stake in 2004.

The affair was satirised in the *Yes, Prime Minister* episode "Man Overboard".

Source (edited): "http://en.wikipedia.org/wiki/Westland_affair"